Are you a new mum and do you feel your dreams of winning the world for Christ are over? Then this book is for you. It is inspirational, practical and refreshingly honest. As you turn the pages you will find yourself becoming excited about the new challenges that motherhood offers you. Buy it. Read it. You will love it!

Mary Pytches, mum, grandmother, author, speaker and counsellor

Whether you're nursing a baby through the night, tempering a toddler tantrum or helping out with homework, this amazing book is a gift to any woman working out what life looks like for a 'missional mum'. Encouraging, insightful and honest, Joy and Anna unpack biblical truths, share the testimonies of a range of women, and talk candidly of their own personal struggles on this important topic. Ordinary Mum, Extraordinary Mission is written by sisters in the trenches – who live it, get it and have wisdom for your journey. A must-read.

Jo Saxton, mum, author, pastor and speaker

Women are God's chosen weapons to bring his kingdom on the earth. This is a thrilling revisit of God's kingdom coming through mothers who hear him and follow. If you want to use your own life, in all its glorious chaos, to change the world, read this book and then do what God tells you!

Danielle Strickland, mum, author, speaker and Salvation Army officer

D1332138

ORDINARY MUM
EXTRAORDINARY
MISSION

ANNA FRANCE-WILLIAMS & JOY FRENCH

ORDINARY
MUM
_EXTRA_ORDINARY
MISSION

SHARING GOD'S LOVE
IN EVERYDAY LIFE

ivp

INTER-VARSITY PRESS
Norton Street, Nottingham NG7 3HR, England
Email: ivp@ivpbooks.com
Website: www.ivpbooks.com

First published 2013

British Library Cataloguing in Publication Data
A catalogue record for this book is available from the British Library.

ISBN: 978–1–78359–024–7

Set in Dante 12/15pt
Typeset in Great Britain by CRB Associates, Potterhanworth, Lincolnshire
Printed in Great Britain by Ashford Colour Press Ltd, Gosport, Hampshire

Inter-Varsity Press publishes Christian books that are true to the Bible and that communicate
the gospel, develop discipleship and strengthen the church for its mission in the world.

Inter-Varsity Press is closely linked with the Universities and Colleges Christian Fellowship, a
student movement connecting Christian Unions in universities and colleges throughout Great
Britain, and a member movement of the International Fellowship of Evangelical Students.
Website: www.uccf.org.uk

CONTENTS

ACKNOWLEDGMENTS

Anna and Joy would like to acknowledge the following:
God, who wants to be known, desires to demonstrate love and chooses to use the likes of us to get the work done. This book was a big assignment, but God provided a great team and for this we are grateful:

All the amazing mums (and dads) who gave us interviews and filled out our extensive questionnaire. Thanks for sharing your journeys with such honesty. We couldn't include you all in the book, but your stories and wisdom have enriched our experience of mission.

Those who read the manuscript and gave us such valuable feedback: Ruth Bushyager, Mary Pytches, Anna Robinson, Hannah Peck and Louie van der Hart.

Sam Parkinson, our editor, and the team at IVP for turning the idea of this book into reality.

Anna would like to acknowledge the following:
My children, Eliana and Micah, two little cheeky souls whose winning smiles alone open great conversations and broker new friendships. Thank you for giving me this incredible opportunity to give other mums a voice and to inspire mission in all of us.

My parents, Esther and Ken, who always welcomed my friends and created a context where Jesus was celebrated and love was shown.

I couldn't have written this book without the support of my husband, Azariah, my reality check and metaphorical external hard drive when my brain felt overloaded and my eyeballs were buffering.

The incredible Life Villages (read chapter 9 for details) whose investment of money, time and love kept us on track and motivated.

I am grateful to Ewa, our angel, who loved our children and nurtured their imaginations.

My fifty faithful friends of prayer who rode in as the cavalry when I felt ambushed by despair, lassoed self-doubt, dusted me down and got me back on the horse to ride the final stretch with hope.

Joy would like to acknowledge the following:
My children, Isaac, Caleb and Moses: you are a joy to me every day – you crazy boys! We're on this journey together and it's a brilliant adventure. My prayer is that you would go deeper and further with Jesus than I have yet been.

My husband, Clynt, who has shown love and patience during the writing of this book, and has motivated and challenged me to live these words out. Thanks for making me laugh and keeping it real.

My mum, Carol, for showing me what it means to be a good and faithful servant, and for your constant example of kindness and generosity.

My nana, Rachel, and my aunty, Marjorie, who are no longer with us, but whose love, generosity, sense of fun and baking skills built this girl some sure foundations in the hardest of times.

Huge thanks go to those who have supported us with prayer, finance, shoulders to cry on and wise counsel while I have been writing this book – you have blessed us beyond measure.

Thanks also to the sisterhood of fabulous women who have championed, been cheerleaders, prayed and fed me cake over the years. You are all an inspiration, but particular thanks have to go to Milly and Lizzy who have walked the longest journey of faithful friendship, encouragement and laughter.

Lastly, thanks to Mike and Sally Breen who originally taught me about 'Oikos' and 'family on mission' in both spoken word and life lived over many years. Thank you for your wisdom and example.

INTRODUCTION

School runs, a thousand packed lunches, play dates, date nights, nappy changes, nose wipes, church meetings, homework diaries, football, work deadlines, bedtime stories, Bible studies, nightmare soothing, supermarket runs, peacekeeping, juice and biscuits, youth groups, park trips, the runs, toddler groups, discipling, disciplining, coffee drinking, mum's taxi, friend listening, potty training, kiss it better. These are our lives. Are they anything like yours?

Let us introduce ourselves. Anna is married to Azariah and they are the proud parents of Eliana (aged three) and Micah (one). Joy is married to Clynt and their children are Isaac (aged thirteen), Caleb (eleven), and Moses (three). We both work alongside our husbands developing churches in urban priority areas. For Anna, this is in London, and for Joy this is in Sheffield.

This book is all about living as a missional mum. Mission is about making Jesus known in the world around us. It is about joining in with God's missionary purposes which concern the entire transformation of the earth, the coming of his kingdom, redeeming humanity and building the church.[1]

We realize that the word 'mission' can be intimidating. It conjures up images of traditional missionaries getting on a boat, sailing away to far-flung countries with only a suitcase, and preaching the gospel to the locals. Perhaps you think mission is only for 'special' Christians who are extra holy or know their Bible really well. Many of us feel that we are just about managing to survive each day, caring for our children and looking after ourselves. 'Doing' mission on top of that might sound like a burden, perhaps even an impossibility. We don't consider we're up to the job or we feel guilty about not doing enough to serve God. It's discouraging and often isolating, particularly if we're part of a small church.

If any of that chimes with you then we hope this book will renew your passion to serve God right where you are. We want to invite you to explore what mission looks like for the normal mum with small children. We want to share the stories of some of those who have begun to boldly go, so that together we can forge a road ahead.

The call to live a missional life means that we look to intentionally share the love of Jesus wherever and with whoever we find ourselves.

This could mean that you, like Helen and her family, try to be a blessing to your difficult neighbour by baking cakes, shovelling snow from her path and mending her fence.

It could mean that you, like Deb, start praying for a sceptical friend who isn't a Christian. Shortly after this, Deb's friend encountered Jesus and, together with her husband, became a Christian.

It could mean that you, like Sheryl, welcome a teenager from your neighbourhood into your home for a cup of tea and a chat about Jesus, even when she is high on drugs. Over time, Sheryl's friend became drug-free and wanted to get baptized.

What might it mean for you?

In this book we explore not only the outward challenges of mission but also the foundations that need to be in place to give mission a strong base: our marriages, our own characters and our family cultures. We are honest about our struggles too: the challenges of carving out time to rest, of learning to work well with others and of juggling the many parts of a missional family life. The 'Tales from the frontline' between chapters are full of incredible wisdom from other mums who are living out the ideas in this book.

There are many exciting adventures ahead for each of us as we embrace God's call to be ourselves and share his love right where we are.

We hope you will be encouraged as you explore what mission looks like for your family in this season of your life, even if it's something you've never thought about before. We pray that you will find ideas to put into practice, stories to make you laugh, Bible passages to challenge you and inspiration from the journeys of those who have blazed a trail.

More than anything, we hope this book will inspire you, showing you that there is a way for you, wherever you are and whatever your circumstances, to live a life that shares God's incredible love with those who have not yet encountered him. We know that, as you begin this journey, you and those around you will be changed beyond recognition as God's transformative power is at work. Let's go!

Anna and Joy

1. HELP! MY CALLING GOT SHRUNK IN THE WASH!

By Joy

Therefore, since we are surrounded by such a great cloud of
witnesses, let us throw off everything that hinders and the sin that
so easily entangles. And let us run with perseverance the race
marked out for us.
(Hebrews 12:1)

Back when I was a teenager, I had great plans for how my ministry was going to develop. I was going to write my first book before I turned nineteen. After studying theology at university, I was going to take the Christian world by storm. I would get ordained, do radical youth work that pushed the boundaries, get married young, pop out four children, and live a shiny, happy life.

I was among the first generation of young people to be touched by Soul Survivor, a festival that aims to inspire and encourage teenagers to live as disciples of Jesus. I utterly loved hearing preaching that was filled with passion and grace, and I and my friends had deep encounters with God, receiving healing and freedom through the power of the Holy Spirit. I was brimming over with confidence and vision. On arriving at university in Sheffield, I joined a large and exciting church. In my second year, I remember walking home from a church meeting passionately singing the Delirious? song, 'History Maker':

I'm gonna be a history maker in this land,
I'm gonna be a speaker of truth to all mankind,
I'm gonna stand, I'm gonna run
Into your arms, into your arms again.
(Extract taken from the song 'History Maker' by Martin Smith.
Copyright © 1996 Curious? Music/Kingsway songs.)

God was gracious despite the arrogance of my youth, and many of the things I dreamed about happened. I took biblical studies at university. I became a youth worker. I got married young (twenty-one), and I have three lovely boys now. All good, but here's the thing – what happens to dreams, calling and vision when you go from being a single twenty-year-old, with the world stretching out before you, to a married, twenty-three-year-old, sleep-deprived mother, with a mountain of washing, a steep mortgage and a puking baby?

Don't get me wrong. I was so grateful for the blessings God had showered upon me. I had grown up with just my mum, without brothers and sisters, and I had longed to be part of a family. In many ways, I now had everything I had always wanted, but how can you be used powerfully in God's kingdom when all you can think about is the next feed and whether you have puréed enough pear to last the week?

As a young mum, it was as though I had entered a different atmosphere from my early days as an only child, often sur-rounded by adults. Here I was, beginning the life I had dreamed of, but feeling ill-equipped and unsure of myself.

My faith and the church culture I was a part of had taught me that God loved me completely, and could do all things – so why didn't he answer my prayers for my baby to sleep through the night?

Even during my first pregnancy, I had attended conferences and meetings that had filled me with vision, passion and excitement to do great things with and for God, and yet, when Isaac was three months old and I was asked if I would speak at a youth conference,

I declined. I didn't feel I could bear to be away from my boy for an hour-long seminar. And I couldn't prepare for it: my head was full with the massive life transition I was experiencing. I had no space to think about youth work – I didn't care at all about those things that I had been so passionate about only months before. This shocked and unsettled me.

My husband Clynt and I had always gone to church on a Sunday night – it was an exciting and dynamic time in the life of our church. Each week there was a sense that God was on the move, changing people's lives. After church, we had hordes of friends back to our house, where we drank tea, ate chips, and dreamed dreams late into the night. It was a life-changing time for us. We had brilliant friends, a vibrant community and a sense of purpose.

When Isaac was born, we proudly took him to church for the first few weeks. We were some of the first in our friendship group to have a baby, and we loved to show our little bundle off, but breastfeeding was difficult in the middle of the brightly lit sports centre where our church met. Isaac was sickly, constantly throwing up all over us. I had envisioned myself enjoying worshipping God as my baby slept sweetly in his car seat. Instead I was harassed and angry, as my husband and friends worshipped alongside me, blissfully unaware of my angst.

As Isaac got older, it became time for him to have a bedtime routine. As all new parents know, trying to crack a sleep routine is the holy grail of early parenthood. But once I got Isaac going to bed in the evenings, I knew that it was time to admit defeat on the evening church front.

Our friends would still come back to our house after church, full of dreams and visions, but I did not know how to be enthusiastic and passionate alongside them, because I felt left behind. Grateful, and content with my lovely boy and the family life we were embarking on, but left behind by the world of dreams and visions, because how can you go anywhere and do anything for Jesus when the baby has to be in bed by seven o'clock?

My situation then – learning how to be an adult at the same time as learning how to be a parent – may be different from yours. Yet the same central issue remains: how do we pursue the dreams and calling that God has given us among the challenges, complexity and responsibilities that life as a parent brings?

Game on: The challenges

In this book we want to explore how we lay deep foundations in our character and relationships and live open-hearted lives of love that share the good news of Jesus. The challenges, as we navigate the twin terrains of building our family life and pursuing our calling, are many. In the day-to-day graft of parenthood we may find ourselves in unfamiliar territory in all of our relationships, including our relationship with God. Our minds and bodies can feel overwhelmed, invaded by exhaustion and the never-ending to-do list. The challenge of working out how to bring together our professional skills, our gifts and calling, and our role as a parent and a marriage partner can feel insurmountable. Even the idea that parenthood could be part of God's calling for your life may be a completely alien concept, as one mum explains:

> I have to say that, growing up, being a mum was not something I thought about a great deal and I certainly didn't feel it was my 'mission' or 'calling'. I graduated from university and was on the hunt for my career – something I could get my teeth stuck into and spend the rest of my working life doing. It took a while, but I found my niche, working in the NHS as a manager. I loved it. At the time, many of my peers couldn't understand the passion I and my husband had for work, but we felt strongly called to the workplace. Many of my friends at this stage were having babies and, to be honest, I loved their kids, but the thought of baby groups, being at home, raising kids . . . frankly, it scared me. I couldn't comprehend the 'baby group' experience; it was just not my bag!
>
> After being married for six years, however, we decided we really wanted to start a family. It was the kind of desire that

comes out of nowhere, for no particular reason. I became
pregnant and we had our first daughter in 2010. She is amazing.
However, I found the transition out of work into motherhood
challenging. Here I was at home, in baby groups, up to my
elbows in nappies and, also, on my own a lot. I just didn't know
what to do. It was as if overnight my 'calling' had been changed,
switched, and I have to be honest: I didn't have a clue what the
new calling looked like.
(Emma, mum to Esther, three, and Charlotte, nine months)

Each of us comes into motherhood differently, and we all have
a variety of skills, talents and passions that we invested in before
we had children. Whatever our lives looked like then, parenthood will change us. How can we begin to make sense of those
changes? How might we begin to see God at work in our own
lives, and in the lives of those around us?

We all know how utterly exhausting and impossible it is to try
to 'have it all' and to be it all. Each of us has only one life, and
we might wonder whether it is possible to bring together our
many roles and responsibilities so that we can create a family life
that functions well and also creates fertile ground for the
kingdom of God to extend around and through us.

Living a missional family life

This book looks at how we build a family life that provides a solid
base for us to love, serve and share Jesus with those around us
– and that is 'real-world proof'. We're going to be exploring some
of the life values that underpin the choices that we make. We're
going to think through what mission is, who we are doing
mission with, and how we might best live missionally in our
context. Our hope is that you will finish this book with a deeper
passion to serve God fully in the midst of family life, and also
with a deep appreciation of your own family – who you are, the
skills that God has equipped you with, and the unique and
beautiful place that your family occupies in the kingdom of God.

A missionary call

We are going to explore the call of God upon all of our lives.

For some of us, this last statement may feel like an exciting rallying call to 'boldly go'. For others, it may cause deep fear and anxiety. We may never have had that 'bolt from the blue' when we felt a strong sense of calling to set up a new project, develop a ministry or pursue a career. Nevertheless, our lives may have been characterized by long and faithful service in the workplace, the home and the church. Whatever our perception of how God has led us to the place we are now, we must recognize that he has plans and purposes for his people (Jeremiah 29:11) even though we may each live this out differently.

As mums, when we survey the wreckage of our lounge each day at teatime and scale the mountain face of exhaustion that bedtime entails, the idea of popping out when the kids are settled in bed to help lead a Bible study, or spend time with a lonely person in the neighbourhood, might make us want to laugh or cry (or both). When I first began writing this book, a close friend who isn't a Christian bought me a fridge magnet that depicts a typical 1950s housewife. Printed on it is the slogan: 'I wanted to change the world, but I couldn't find a babysitter.'

This is how many of us feel about the challenge of living a missional life. We know our comfort zone – come seven o'clock at night, it's the sofa, the remote control and a bar of chocolate. But isn't there more to following Jesus than this? Jesus never said that following him would be an easy or safe option. Are we prepared to entrust ourselves to him and begin his bold and adventurous journey?

It is certain that all mums have a call upon their lives to parent. God has charged us with the responsibility of shaping lives that will in turn shape and change the world of the future. In this sense, all of us who are parents are world changers.

It is also certain that we are all called, whatever our context, to live lives that are missional.

Let's unpack exactly what that means.

In Matthew 28, as Jesus is about to ascend to heaven, he speaks out these words to his disciples:

All authority in heaven and on earth has been given to me. Therefore go and make disciples of all nations, baptising them in the name of the Father and of the Son and of the Holy Spirit, and teaching them to obey everything I have commanded you. And surely I am with you always, to the very end of the age. (Matthew 28:18–20)

The word 'mission' comes from the Latin *missio*, which means 'to send'. *Missio* is the task undertaken by the *apostoloi*, which in New Testament Greek means 'sent ones'. Just as Jesus sent the twelve apostles out to disciple all nations in the words of the Great Commission above, so he sends each of us today into our homes, communities and workplaces.

It is a commonplace Christian first-world problem to spend a great deal of time ruminating over our 'calling'. We ask questions about whether we're called to this career or that, to work or stay at home, to worship in a particular Christian community, live in a particular area, minister to a particular people group. These are valid questions, worthy of prayer and exploration. But what we see in the Gospels is that Jesus primarily called his disciples to do two things: to follow him (be a disciple) and to make disciples. We are called to be discipling disciples; that is, followers who lead others into a life of discipleship. This can be our only starting point as we seek to unpack how the life of a missional mother might look.

In Luke 9 and 10, Jesus sends out first his twelve disciples, then seventy-two of his fledgling followers. He gives them scant instructions: they are to take nothing for the journey ahead, but they are to go to new communities and share the good news of the kingdom of God, praying for the sick and casting out demons. Where they are welcomed, they must stay; where they are refused welcome, they must leave. I love the way that Jesus responds when his excited disciples return, full of amazement at all they have seen and been involved in. We read:

> The seventy-two returned with joy and said, 'Lord, even the demons submit to us in your name.'
> He replied, 'I saw Satan fall like lightning from heaven . . .'
> At that time Jesus, full of joy through the Holy Spirit, said, 'I praise you, Father, Lord of heaven and earth, because you have hidden these things from the wise and learned, and revealed them to little children. Yes, Father, for this was your good pleasure.'
> (Luke 10:17–18, 21 NIV1984)

This blows my mind. Then and now, Jesus chooses to entrust the sharing of his kingdom, his love, his character and his reputation to people like us. Could Jesus impact the whole of humanity with his glory in a heartbeat? Yes! And one day he will. But for now, he loves to watch his followers as they do what they were designed to do: follow and lead others, be disciples who disciple – ordinary people, living ordinary lives that have been touched by an extraordinary God.

This book is all about encouraging each of us, whatever our gifts, calling or circumstances to get off the starting blocks and begin to share Jesus the best way we can. Let me give you some examples of what this might look like:

When Isaac was a baby, I was incredibly blessed by the older ladies of the church who ran a 'meals ministry' and provided us with a cooked meal every day for a fortnight after his birth. This practical expression of God's love blew us away. When we moved across the city and many of our friends were having babies, we resolved that as a community we would roll out this provision to all in our friendship group. Those who weren't Christians quickly became both recipients and providers of fantastic meals, and many people experienced the love of God in action. This was a simple and yet incredibly effective way to meet a need and develop community through practical service.

My fab friend Milly has been part of a group of parents who are committed to praying for and serving their children's infant school. These parents are not only praying for the school, but are also actively looking for ways that they can be a blessing to the wider school community. Alongside weekly prayer meetings, they take prayer requests from teachers each term, offer prayer for parents in the playground, run stalls at school fairs, show prospective parents around the school, sit on the board of governors and make meals for staff when it's parents' evening. I regularly drive past this school in the morning, and it is not unusual to see parents praying for each other in the street!

When my friend Abi moved onto an urban estate, she discovered that there was no local toddler group. Undaunted, she gathered some other Christian mum friends, and began a coffee morning in the local pub. She explains:

> Our Coffee Morning meets once a week in the function room of a very 'local' pub on our council estate. We have up to twenty adults each week, most of whom are mums like me with varying numbers of children, but we also have dads, single women, grandparents and, perhaps most delightfully, random old ladies from down the road who just like coming to see the babies. Incidentally, we very deliberately called it a 'Coffee Morning with Playgroup' rather than just a playgroup, since one of our aims was to meet as wide a range of people as possible and I didn't want to put up unnecessary barriers to anyone. Occasionally we do a themed activity, but usually we just lay out a bunch of toys (the vast majority of which are donated), provide a little something that I've baked every week, and then the Christians in the group just make a concerted effort to welcome anyone and everyone who comes in the door.
> (Abi, mum to Barney, aged two)

There are so many creative ways that we can share the love of God with those we naturally see every day at work, at toddler groups, at the school gates and on the street. People everywhere are searching for love, meaning and acceptance in this challenging world. Even if we can make just one of these ideas work, we can make a real difference. Can we offer ourselves as the hands and feet of Jesus where we are right now?

Should I stay or should I go?

Jesus' call on his followers in the Gospels was to first come to him as willing followers (disciples), and then to 'go'!

Did you know that it says 'Go!' in the Bible 1,542 times, and 'Stay' only sixty-two times?

Living a missionary lifestyle feels very much like 'going', and yet life as a parent often feels as though it's about 'staying'. As families, the reality is that we are called to go, that is, to step out in mission, even if that means that we physically stay in the same place – although it may not. We find a complex tension here, between the 'go' aspect of mission and the tendency for parents to want to 'stay' to protect family life. This is a tension that we cannot and should not ignore.

It is tempting when we find tensions between theological ideas to decide that it's best to just 'not go there'. This is understandable, especially when as mums we are often fully occupied with whether there's milk in the fridge and toilet roll in the bathroom; and yet often it's in the confusing, messy places that we can unearth profound truths.

These places of tension, which we find as we seek to plumb the depths in our exploration of God, can be good and healthy. It is the same as we try to explore the tension between the 'Go' of mission and the 'Stay' of parenting. If all we can think about is the need to 'go', to be actively pursuing mission whatever the costs, we run the risk of letting things slide in our families, causing them to feel second place to the 'things of God'. Likewise, if all we think of is the need to 'stay', in order to protect our children from the costs of radical discipleship, we run the risk of raising pampered, consumer Christian children.

STAY ←————————————————→ GO

If we drew a continuum for ourselves with 'Stay' at one end, and 'Go' at the other, we might quickly be able to locate our natural tendency. This is a helpful process, as it enables us to think about the challenges for our own families right now. It may be that you need to pull back on church meetings, so that you can spend time with your children in the evenings, investing in their character and relationship with God. It may be that as a family there are new missional frontiers on the horizon that you can begin to explore together.

How can we talk about what God calls us to do as he sends us out in mission and as he calls us to parent our children? We fall into thinking that it's family *or* mission, or even family *and* mission, but perhaps the most helpful language we can use is to say family *on* mission.

So what does *that* look like?
Let's start with exactly where you are right now. You're a busy mum who wants to follow God – that's all I have to go on, because all mums are busy, and I guess if you didn't want to follow God you probably wouldn't be reading this book. You may have one child or several; you may or may not have a partner. You might fill your days working at home, or in a workplace. Whatever life looks like for you right now, let's start there.

A life of mission cannot be about God adding in a gazillion extra tasks into our already sanity-stretchingly busy lives. Is that really how Jesus, who promised to lead us in 'the unforced rhythms of grace', works (Matthew 11:28–30, MSG)? Mission is less about engaging in a specific set of activities, and much more about developing a mindset; less about tasks, and more about relationships.

God is by nature a missionary God: the Father sends the Son into the world, and the Son and the Father send the Spirit. God is on a mission; it's who he is. This, then, is how a missionary mindset (as opposed to a task list) needs to permeate our thinking. Wherever we go, whatever we do, whoever we are with, we are the sent ones of Jesus, ambassadors of his love, grace and transforming power in a messed-up and broken world.

The starting point has to be our minds. This is the place where so many battles are won and lost. There is so much in everyday life that can drag us down. From sickness and stress to toil and tiredness, it's easy to forget that we are equipped by the Holy Spirit and sent out as bearers of good news. I was recently at a Christian conference and was encouraged when the speaker shared that we are 'carriers of the presence of Jesus'. He challenged us to think this way as we go about our ordinary, everyday lives.

A couple of weeks later, I was in a shopping centre, rushing around getting tasks done. My shoulders were down, and no doubt stress registered on my face as I considered the ratio of jobs completed to childcare time remaining.

Suddenly, I thought to myself, 'Here, right now, I am a carrier of the presence of Jesus.' This changed things. I raised my head, and looked around at the people in front of me, faces tired and careworn, just like mine had been. Everyone was rushing around, busy and preoccupied. I was reminded of Jesus' reaction in Matthew's Gospel: 'When he saw the crowds, he had compassion on them, because they were harassed and helpless, like sheep without a shepherd' (Matthew 9:36). I began to observe people differently, each of these passers-by, utterly beloved by the King of kings. My shoulders lifted. I smiled and made eye contact with people as we passed. I no longer felt bowed down with cares. I could sense God's desire to break through the ordinary and humdrum in all of our lives with the revelation of his extra-ordinary presence.

Mission has to be about God's mission, not ours. Isn't this a relief? Jesus was very clear about how he conducted his life. We read in John, 'Very truly I tell you, the Son can do nothing by himself; he can do only what he sees his Father doing, because whatever the Father does the Son also does' (John 5:19). We are simply called to do the same: joining in where we see that the Father is already at work. Mission is not about me and my agenda. It is about figuring out what part of God's wider mission I can participate in right now.

I recently had an experience that underlined my need to be tuned in to where God is actually at work, rather than where I think he should be. My husband and I were feeling hard-pressed and were trying to think through how we could develop some new work with parents and toddlers on the housing estate we work on. I was already involved in running a toddler group which was in a different neighbourhood, and we wondered if I ought to relinquish responsibility for this group so that there would be time to set up something new. Many of the toys were old and shabby. It was limping along, with a few faithful attenders, and I felt a bit despondent about it. I was going through the motions, turning up at the last minute and not really putting the effort in to make it warm and welcoming.

But out of the blue, a strange change began to take place. New faces began to show up; we received some funding and bought some new equipment, and before I had time to take it in or make any plans, the group had doubled in size. I was the only Christian involved in running the group and, despite my previous sense that it was not a fertile ground for mission, I found that I was increasingly having conversations with the parents about God. The group is still steadily welcoming a stream of new people, and only last week one of the mums asked me if we could set up a 'Messy Church'[2] in her local school. None of this would have happened if I had persisted in trying to develop new things where I thought they ought to be. Instead, God drew me in to an engagement with what he was already doing under my nose.

Part of the challenge is to hold on to the awareness that we are 'carriers of the presence of Jesus' wherever in life we find ourselves. Combining this awareness with a resolve to seek out and be a part of what God is already doing in our home, community, school, workplace and church will lead us into all manner of adventures and exploits.

I love the story of Sarah, who volunteers with her baby son in tow at a project for pregnant refugee women. She explains:

> My son comes with me every week when I volunteer at MRANG (Merseyside Refugee Ante-Natal Support Group). The group is attended by thirty to fifty women and their children at each meeting. Just under half of babies born in the group are the result of rape in war zones; the organization also supports women who've been trafficked or separated from their children. The group does lots of good casework and counselling. We just go in and chat to the women. Having recently had a baby, I can recommend local services to them and occasionally allay fears about interacting with the health service. Especially when he was small, Seb generally loved to be passed around and held. I remember an African lady, who had fled conflict and persecution and been separated from her own children for over ten years, peacefully sitting there, cradling my baby. I also loved seeing the sparkling face of a Rwandan woman playing with Seb. We visited her in a mental health unit after she had tried to take her own life. There's a joy and a normality about bringing a baby with you to these places.
>
> (Sarah, mum to Seb, twenty months)

There are infinite possibilities that open up as we begin to realize that our children can not only come along for the ride, but also be powerfully used by God as we say 'yes' to following him as a family. Whether you are sharing the love and the invitation of Jesus at the school gates, in the community or via a project or at work, trying to live a family life that shares God's love with others may be messy, but will certainly not be dull. Are you ready to embark on this crazy adventure?

Living sacrifices

In many ways, being a parent, while delightful, is a kind of 'death to self'. For Christians, this is not a new idea – in Romans 12 Paul talks of us offering ourselves to God as 'living sacrifices' (v. 1, NIV1984). It can be easy for us to interpret this verse as a challenge to be prepared to give anything up, go anywhere and do anything as we journey with God. Perhaps it's not always so easy to understand it as we think about the sacrifice of ourselves that we make as parents, the sacrifice of sleep, time, energy, relationships, the Saturday morning paper in bed, even our minds and bodies. We all have times when these sacrifices can feel just a little overwhelming.

In the 1950s, one of the first British child psychotherapists, Donald Winnicott, wrote a paper entitled 'Primary Maternal Preoccupation',[3] about the earliest relationship between a mother and her baby. He theorized that a mother's capacity to give herself over, temporarily, to her baby at the very beginning of the infant's life is foundational for the development of the relationship between the mother and baby, and consequently, for the development of the baby's personality. Subsequently, neuroscience research has discovered that, as parents attend to and regulate their baby's emotional states in the early days, neural pathways are laid down in the infant's brain that over time become fixed. (To learn more about this, read the excellent *Why Love Matters: How Affection Shapes a Baby's Brain*, by Sue Gerhardt.[4]) This early relationship between a baby and his or her parents is the foundation upon which the rest of the child's life will be built.

Reflecting on this has helped me to make sense of the kind of sacrifice that Paul is talking about in Romans 12. When the early church was establishing itself, animal sacrifice was an important part of worship for most religions. If anyone wanted to give thanks to God for an important event, or atone for sin and wrongdoing, sacrifice was the way to show commitment to God. For Paul, however, the sacrifice that God loves is not an external show of a dead animal offered up, but rather the internal sacrifice of ourselves to our heavenly Father. An offering of our hearts, our minds, our will, our capacity – our all.

This is such an overwhelming challenge. I once heard a minister put it like this: 'The problem with living sacrifices is that they can walk off the table!' We must choose daily to continue to bring ourselves to God. It can be easy to think that only counts when it is a 'spiritual' act – reading the Bible, prayer or sung worship. I wonder if this is really the case? When nine-month-old Isaac was screaming in the night, and I just didn't think I could deal with it any more, I had to go beyond my pain barrier, push beyond my threshold, in order to give him what he needed. Was this offering of myself to the child that God had given me and called me to care for any less spiritual than standing at the front of church with my arms raised high? At that moment, and at countless others, none of which felt very spiritual, that sacrifice of myself, of my needs and desires, was my 'spiritual act of worship' (Romans 12:1 NIV1984). It was all I had, and that is all that our Father in heaven wants.

As we approach the many challenges involved in living life as a family on mission, it is as though the whole family is climbing up onto the altar. We bring to the table our bleary-eyed, play-dough smudged, rag-tag and bobtailed tribe, and we sit and wonder: What is this going to mean? There is something terri-fyingly real about putting ourselves 'out there', about saying that we, and that means all of us, are in this thing. And yet incredible and beautiful heavenly transactions are occurring as we climb onto that table. The kingdom of God was always meant to be at its most tangible in the hands of little children. Can it be true that the ultimate Father in heaven delights in the messes made by smudges of little hands on the holy table? Can it be that we will be truly liberated when we realize that it is he, not ourselves, who will ultimately keep our children safe? And that the safest place of all to be is in the presence of our heavenly King?

The bigger picture

The verse at the beginning of this chapter talks about 'running the race with perseverance' – this is an apt image for a family on mission. By the time we become parents, we have run a variety of different races – perhaps completing education, embarking on a career, getting involved in church projects and ministries. These will have developed our skills and shaped our character, but compared to the endurance marathon that is family life, they seem like short sprints.

Raising children is an emotional rollercoaster experience. Grafting away as a family at the coalface of mission takes resources that will often far exceed what we can muster in our own strength. It's so important to remember why we are doing all this.

Every child is born to broken parents in this broken world. But, as Christians, we are all called to be builders of the kingdom of God. Jesus talked throughout the Gospels about the 'kingdom of God'. He was clear that this was what he had come to establish. For Christians, this means that we live lives that demonstrate who God is and what it means to live under his good rule and reign.

As parents, building the kingdom in our family life means that we start from the ground up – investing in strong foundations in our relationship with God, in our own character, in our marriages and in our relationship with our children so that ultimately we and they go out into the world equipped to be agents of change, bringers of God's love into the hurting world we all inhabit.

It might be tempting for us, with busy lives, or lots of ideas and plans for the future, to see the daily work of parenting as a spiritually empty space, where we are being held back from all of those other achievements. It is true that this is a time when we make a great many sacrifices and often cannot see the rewards. But as we invest in and grow the bond with our children, we are doing something radical and powerful in the kingdom of

God. We are developing and shaping lives by investing in the foundations of unique individuals, co-creating with God and establishing a future and a destiny for our children and their world, so that God's kingdom will continue to be established down the line of the generations we leave behind. Could this be the ultimate legacy?

Questions for exploration

1. What have been some of the biggest challenges to your faith since becoming a parent?
2. Where would you place yourself on the Stay/Go continuum of missional family life?
3. How might your daily life be impacted by the knowledge that you are a carrier of the presence of Jesus?
4. What are your dreams about how God will use you in this season of your life?

TALES FROM THE FRONTLINE

Louise
(mum to James, eighteen months)

Louise has had ME for nearly six years and is almost entirely house-bound. She is passionate about teaching the Bible and answering the tricky questions of faith. Louise loves to communicate and interact with others through blogging.

I'm a goal-setter, a strategist.

My husband and I were in church ministry and led a biblical theology course together. I called myself a pastor-teacher and evangelist, and began to grow in confidence and plan ahead. And then I had a baby and it all fell apart.

I have ME, a debilitating autoimmune / neurological illness. It had affected my mobility and concentration for several years, but after giving birth it got significantly worse. As a new mum, I found myself unable to walk more than a few metres. Even talking with friends had to be carefully rationed. I could no longer lecture in biblical theology, and I couldn't go to church – I couldn't read anything more than a magazine article. I needed help to look after my beautiful baby boy because I was too weak to carry him and change his nappy. It has been two years now, and although my concentration has improved I am still house-bound, needing to spend most of the day in bed.

I had lost my Plan A. This wasn't Plan B or even Plan C. This was Plan Z. How do you follow a calling when circumstances are beyond your control and it's all gone wrong?

It has not been easy. There are times when it feels, for all my training and ministry background, that I am clinging on to faith by the skin of my teeth.

In the midst of this, God brought Racquel into my life. We needed a nanny; she needed a job.

We were both feeling fairly bruised by life, and in the first month of her employment we bonded over a mutual disapproval of drinking culture and abusive men. I explained (semi-defensively) that, although it was unpopular, I thought the Christian teaching of saving sex for marriage prevented a lot of heartache. To my immense surprise, she agreed and told me that she'd been brought up as a Christian but had since gone against it, which she now regretted.

She had been very honest with me despite not knowing me well, and I didn't know whether to push any further. But then I thought, 'Why not? I'll just ask it.' Tentatively, I said, 'If you don't mind me asking, where does that leave you now in your relationship with God?' She burst into tears, and sobbed, 'I feel like I've lost my way, and I don't know how to get back.'

That was the start of many things: a firm friendship between us; a spiritual journey for Racquel that culminated in her committing her life to God on our landing while James played at our feet and we both wept happy tears. It was also a spiritually healing experience for me. Racquel was the only non-Christian in my life. And God happened to bring us together.

In the midst of my questions about why God had flung me into Plan Z, there was a glimpse of an answer. It was not *the* answer but an encouragement that God was still at work in and through me.

2. MARRIAGE: ROOTS AND FRUITS

By Anna

> *A new command I give you: love one another. As I have loved you,*
> *so you must love one another. By this everyone will know that you*
> *are my disciples, if you love one another.*
> (John 13:34–35)

We were waiting in the doctor's surgery, fingers intertwined, having just had the news confirmed. My tear-stained face was alive with expectation and my body was shaking with adrenalin, delighted and overwhelmed by the news that I was expecting our first child. My husband Azariah's face was burgeoning with pride as he took stock of his new role as father, his arm wrapped protectively around me. Over the next few weeks we began to consider the awesome changes that we were about to face in our marriage of three years. It was no longer just about the two of us.

Writing about marriage, mission and having small children is tricky because our relational contexts are so diverse. Some of us are parenting alone and perhaps longing to get married. Others are married to someone who doesn't share our Christian faith and are working out what it means to parent together. Some of us conceived before or just shortly after getting married so will have little or no experience of marriage pre-children. Others may have adopted or fostered children or waited years (intentionally, or perhaps due to problems conceiving) before having a baby. The way we regard our marriages also varies. Marriage is a struggle for some of us; for others, it is primarily a blessing.

Azariah and I live in London. Our church is on a housing estate and Azariah is the vicar. We are seeking to live missionally as a family with our two children, Eliana, aged three, and Micah, one. We have learned that our marriage needs to be a healthy place from which mission flows. Investing in the unseen aspects of our marriage – our friendship, intimacy and teamwork – strengthens our ability to serve our family and our community. That's why we need to explore marriage when we're looking at mission. It is the bedrock of what we become as a family.

When Azariah and I were engaged I was praying, and I had a picture in my mind of what our marriage would look like – the attributes it needed to develop to be mission-focused and healthy. It is a picture that I think is applicable to all those who want their marriages to be places from which mission flows.

I saw our marriage as two trees planted next to each other with roots that went deep down into the ground to soak up all the goodness in the soil. Our roots needed to be nourished by God if we were to remain healthy.

Our branches were intertwined in places which gave our marriage strength. We were to nurture our marriage through friendship and intimacy and to be a team, serving God together.

There were also branches on each tree that were separate, representing some of the individual callings or ministries God had for us and which we would have to work hard to support each other in.

The branches had people sitting in them, representing the missional reach of our marriage, its 'fruit' – we would be a place of refuge, healing and support to others, including our children, and there would be spiritual fruit which grew as a result of our marriage.

This metaphor of twin trees shows what is needed to make a healthy missional marriage: deep roots in God and strong branches (both intertwined and separate) lead to fruit-bearing. Healthy roots lead to healthy fruits.

Perhaps you are painfully aware of the struggles in your marriage, and because of this your dreams for missional living seem impossible. Maybe you are aware that you have not given your marriage much attention recently. It's easy to get complacent and forget the vital role that our marriages play in enabling mission to flourish. What would it look like if your marriage was a flourishing tree, nourished by God and able to affect those around you?

In this chapter we will consider how our marriages can form a strong foundation for missional living in three areas: nurturing friendship, intimacy and teamwork. These can be under strain when we have young children. Nurturing them is a spiritual act of worship and a way in which, as the verses from John 13 above say, we can love each other and our love can demonstrate our love for Christ to others.

Quality 1: Nurturing friendship

Nurturing friendship in a marriage is a way in which we can demonstrate our love for each other. The idea of our spouse being our best friend is biblical. Proverbs 2:17 speaks of a spouse as an *allup*, a Hebrew word that can be translated as 'special confidante' or 'best friend'. This is a remarkable description of a marriage relationship, considering the way women in biblical times were often seen as their husband's property.[5] Friendship is meant to be central to a marriage, and what friends do best and most naturally is spend time with each other.

Before Azariah and I had children it was much easier to spend time together and do things which best friends do, like quick trips to see the latest film or impromptu visits to the local pizza place. I don't think we realized it then, but those times were like gold dust. Our friendship really cemented. We chatted late into the night, lavished appreciation on one another and had precious moments of brutal honesty about how we were feeling. We also spent a lot of time talking about our hopes and dreams for the future, what we loved, what we hated and what values we wanted our family to prioritize.

When we had Eliana and Micah, our friendship as a couple changed. We went to the cinema less, spent our money on nappies instead of treats, couldn't go out spontaneously for a meal as we had to organize babysitters, and rarely went away for the weekend. Where had those precious moments of talking honestly about our feelings gone? And what happened to those vital conversations about our hopes and dreams for the future? Our time was spent looking after our children and making our life work at a basic level, plus trying to snatch the hard-to-come-by luxury of sleep.

Here's what Iain, dad to nine-month-old Grace, said about how having children affected his marriage: 'I think the biggest adjustment that we have needed to make is that our lives no longer revolve around us. We eat after Grace has been fed and gone to bed, not when we are hungry. When we go out, we plan it around when she will need to feed or sleep.'

The easy thing to do once children come along is to ignore your friendship with your husband and concentrate all your energies on your children. Your relationship then becomes like that of work colleagues rather than a friendship based on love and intimacy. Sound familiar? If friendship is so important, how can we nurture and prioritize it so our marriages flow with love and grace to those around us? Can we imagine the impact that a marriage like this could have on the world – the people that would be drawn towards it, and the strength which it could bring us and our family as we serve our neighbours and those in our sphere of influence?

Prioritizing regular and quality time together has to be the starting place. And this isn't easy. It has taken immense determination for us to carve out time regularly, and we're still struggling with it! Sometimes our marriages need attention, our children are ill, and we have a pressing work or church deadline. How do we decide what is the priority in each situation? I don't think there are easy, formulaic answers. Sometimes we will not get it right. And that's OK. Different families will prioritize in different ways. But we are all called to care for our marriages. Whatever that looks like for us, we have to ensure that our relationship with our spouse stays healthy.

Nicky and Sila Lee, in *The Marriage Book*, say that the three most important things about couples spending regular time together are to plan it, prioritize it and protect it.[6] They recommend that couples should have a regular time every week of at least two hours spent alone together. This could be called a 'date night' or 'marriage time'. Some couples will find this suggestion works. Others may need to improvise around it.

Here's how Louie, mum to Skye, three, and Joseph, one, prioritizes time with her husband:

> We were trying to go out once a week together by getting a babysitter but sometimes we were just too tired and didn't feel like it. So we decided to have a weekly evening in where we relax, watch a film and eat a takeaway. Sometimes we get a babysitter during the day for a couple of hours so that we can go out for coffee and have a proper chat. It's important to be creative and not get stuck in a rut. You need to hold on to what's important – your marriage.

A regular date night may feel totally impossible for you at the moment. If you have a small baby then you may not have pre-dictable 'free' time, but perhaps you could plan an evening to get a takeaway, chat instead of watch TV, and enjoy each other's company. If you have children who are still awake and around doing homework or playing on computer games at 10pm then getting a regular babysitter for date night might be the best idea. How can you and your husband better plan, prioritize and protect your time together?

What is the missional fruit of marriages like this? By prioritizing quality time together, whatever that looks like in this season of life, we will be making an investment in our marriage that will strengthen our friendship with each other and therefore enable us to be a stronger base for mission. What do you and your husband enjoy doing together that is fun and life-giving? What makes you relax, laugh and unwind? Azariah and I are big fans of coffee shops and bookshops. When we make time for these things we create capacity and energy in our marriage to be able to serve others without resentment. The twin trees of our marriage begin to develop strong branches which can support the weight of the needs of others. When Azariah and I get our coffee shop fix we are more likely to have the capacity as a couple to host a mulled wine and mince pies party for our neighbours at Christmas, or to stop to encourage a friend we meet at the supermarket who is having a tough time. We also become the kind of family that others want to be around. There's something magnetizing about families who enjoy life; other people are drawn to them and this provides opportunities to show just how wonderfully life-giving our God is!

Spending time together also creates an opportunity for us to remember what our vision and values are as a couple and how they might impact our mission as a family. Do we want to be a family that is particularly hospitable or generous or peaceful? In the season of having young children it is easy to lose sight of why God brought us together in the first place. When you hang out together it opens up time to dream and think about the ways in which God may want to use your gifts as a couple and as a family.

When Azariah and I got engaged we put together a list of values which we wanted to prioritize in our relationship. Since having children, we have had to revisit that list and work out what the values look like in our new context and with the mission opportunities we have. For example, one of our values is stewardship. We want to be generous and wise with the money and possessions God has given us; this is part of the mission God has called us to. For instance, we have decided to sponsor a child from Rwanda through the charity Compassion[7] in order to provide for her basic needs and schooling – something we can involve our children in. Another way we express this value of stewardship is by purchasing thoughtful gifts for others for no particular reason. We also lend and give away books to people that we hope will prompt them to think about faith. These actions, stemming from our values, are a way in which we can apply Jesus' command to 'love one another' (John 13:34–35). We hope and pray that, by doing this, God's kingdom will grow. When we decide as a couple to be wise and generous with our money it prompts questions in others. It also gives us the opportunity to model and explain how, as a family, we trust God to provide for us and we use money generously because it is a gift from him.

Every family is different and our values will mean that we impact the world differently for God. Our friends, Tony and Claire, parents to Josiah, three, and Myla, six months, consistently live out the principles of environmentally friendly, ethically conscious living. To them, looking after God's world and valuing the needs of the poor, for instance through buying Fairtrade products, is a way to live missionally as a family of four. Their choices influence not just their own children but also all those in their community who come into contact with them. They have challenged us by the way they live and we have changed some of our buying habits as a result.

One couple we know place great value on global mission and have a world map in their house which they use when praying with their two sons for other countries, including the persecuted church. Child-rearing can be all-consuming and we can often find it difficult to maintain our shared interests. But these things make us distinct and are often the areas which God wants to use as a channel of his blessing to others. Making the time to keep our values and vision alive will keep us going in the difficult times and provide an opportunity to meet those who are not yet

Christians. Our branches will be strengthened and our twin trees will flourish.

Now may be a good time to sit down and revisit some of the values and the vision you had at the beginning of your marriage or to consider these things for the first time. Below is a list of twelve values which could help to formulate your vision for family life and how you want to serve others. Pick those that fit your family best. You may think of others that are not on the list that you want to add. Pray with and talk to your partner about ways in which these values can be applied in your family and touch those around you.

- Generosity
- Hospitality
- Justice
- Compassion
- Prayerfulness
- Creativity
- Honesty
- Humility
- Forgiveness
- Kindness
- Peace
- Courage

Quality 2: Nurturing intimacy

His mouth is sweetness itself;
    he is altogether lovely.
This is my beloved, this is my friend,
    daughters of Jerusalem.
(Song of Songs 5:16)

Building intimacy in marriage is vital when there are so many things that can divide and separate us: work schedules, tiredness, practical chores or perhaps a temptation to indulge in flirtation with someone else. If we want our marriages to be a missional base from which we work and go out into the world, then we need to be totally committed to each other. You may think that sex is irrelevant to mission, but sex builds emotional closeness and this strengthens our marriage (see 1 Corinthians 7:5). A strong marriage is one which can stay intact when faced with the often complex and draining challenges of missional living.

Azariah and I were virgins when we got married. This was an achievement, but it also means that six years later we still have L-plates on. I'm going to be honest here in the hope that my story will help others to realize they are not alone. Our sex life hasn't been a walk in the park. For some couples, things work out without complication. For me, sex is a bit like exercise: I know it's good for something, but it feels like an effort to get into the right frame of mind. Azariah is short-sighted and I'm long-sighted, which probably didn't help our attempts at lovemaking. Neither of us could quite see the other in the dark and it was all fumbles, uncoordinated limbs, more ouch than oooh. It was overwhelmingly humbling to see that not one but two children resulted from our confused and, at times, tearful bedtime antics.

I don't think we're alone in our struggles for intimacy. For some of us, the struggles have always been there, and for others they began once children arrived. Many husbands and wives agree that their sex life suffers as a result of having children. In the weeks after I gave birth to my daughter I could barely sit down from the soreness of the forceps and episiotomy. My nipples were bleeding, I caught several infections and I was gulping down the painkillers like sweets. Was I desperate to slip on a lacy negligee and engage in a bit of nooky at bedtime? I think not.

Months later, the sleep-interrupted nights had taken their toll and 'I'm too tired' became the familiar phrase Azariah heard just as his hand slid hungrily towards me, his engine beginning to rev up. For those of us with a number of children, our bodies can feel less sexual and more like climbing frames, clambered on, pulled, clawed at, dribbled and vomited on, and cuddled to varying degrees.

For too long this level of honest engagement with the subject of sex has been a hidden corner in the lives of the married. How can we model and instil truth into our children if our fears in this area resist investigation? Our sex life will never be perfect, but it's ours, and our commitment determines that we keep on practising this most complex of duets and celebrating this gift that God has given us for marriage.

Colin, dad to Sarah, six, James, four, and Ellie, two, said this:

> I was shocked that our relationship changed from the moment Mary became pregnant. Having less sex was definitely a big deal for me. After the birth, all three of us were absolutely tired out. But for Mary and me, that tiredness seemed to define the whole season of having kids, which was almost eight years. It meant we needed a whole new way of functioning in our relationship.

If what Colin says is true, where do we start when it comes to navigating our sex lives in the context of having small children?

Let's start with looking at why sex is important in a marriage. I found this image helpful, from Tim Keller, likening sex in a marriage to the oil needed in an engine:

> Time, children, illness, and age all bring changes that may require creative, disciplined responses to rebuild a sexual intimacy that was easier at an earlier time. If you don't confront and adapt to these changes they'll erode your sex life. Kathy and I often liken sex in a marriage to oil in an engine – without it, the friction between all the moving parts will burn out the motor. Without joyful, loving sex, the friction in a marriage will bring about anger, resentment, hardness and disappointment. Rather than being the commitment glue that

holds you together, it can become a force to divide you. Never give up working on your sex life.[8]

'Commitment glue' is needed when you have small children. Commitment glue is needed to build a strong foundation for mission in our families; to stick together and persevere when we're ill; to see how God is using us when we're under financial pressure or struggling at work. Commitment to each other is what God designed for marriage and what Jesus advocates in Matthew 19:1–6. I want my marriage to be well-oiled. I want to protect it. I want to choose intimacy over resentment, sacrifice over selfishness, and commitment over apathy. How can we prioritize intimacy in our marriages?

One way is by putting it in the diary. When I first heard someone recommend 'putting sex in the diary' I flinched. Having grown up on a diet of rom-coms and Hollywood films, the idea seemed ridiculous. I am sure some couples are at it like rabbits as soon as the children are in bed, but for me, putting 'it' in the diary means an intentional decision to prioritize intimacy no matter how tired I am or how I am feeling. What puts you in the mood for sex? Since having children there have been times when Azariah has surprised me by doing all the washing up and I have pounced on him, much to *his* surprise! For others, quality time together or a thoughtful gift could be the thing that ignites passion. Prioritizing intimacy isn't just about the act of sex though. Touching, holding, kissing and eye contact can also bring us closer emotionally – and often lead to sex.

Sara, mum to Caleb, four, Seth, two, and Hannah, nine months, said this: 'Intimacy is a constant challenge, especially post childbirth. Being open and honest with each other about how you feel is crucial. My husband and I have very different needs in that area and compromise is necessary. We manage by putting sex in the diary so we both know what to expect.'

Organizing time away as a couple can be a great way to build intimacy. Romance blooms when we are on a break together.

There is space to be spontaneous. We can give each other focused attention without having to stick to our children's routine.

Emma, mum to Evelyn, sixteen months, said, 'We have much less "romantic" time together now. It's hard to find an opportunity for intimacy when you've got a baby in the house. We've had to make deliberate plans to go off somewhere for a couple of days, for occasions such as birthdays and anniversaries, so that we can still have quality time together.'

To plan time away, we need support from friends or family who can babysit. This can be a challenge, especially if your parents or in-laws are not around. Is there someone you know and trust who might enjoy looking after your child or children? You may not be able to manage a night away, but perhaps you could start with a morning or a day? If no-one comes to mind, this is something you could pray about together.

When there is intimacy and commitment in our marriage it becomes a place of incredible strength and joy. Can we imagine the possibilities that can flow from these kinds of marriages? Can we begin to see the needs around us and reach out together to be a blessing? This might mean praying together daily for a friend who is searching for God or who is ill with cancer; inviting work colleagues round to watch a sports game; deciding as a couple to have a month where we encourage someone every day in person or by text message. These actions may seem small but can have a significant effect on those around us.

Quality 3: Effective teamwork: parenting together

'Love cares more for others than for self . . .' (1 Corinthians 13:4 MSG).

Let's return for a moment to the image of the twin trees. One of the distinctive features of these trees was the combination of intertwined branches and separate branches. When we marry we don't leave our individuality at the door. We become a team. There are things God calls us to do jointly and also things he calls us to do separately. How do we navigate all these things and work out what it means to be a team working together under God? As an effective parenting team we will disciple our children together, care for each partner's needs, juggle our different work responsibilities, handle conflicts and seek to live missionally. Where do we start? We learn how to love each other with the self-sacrifical love of Christ, as outlined in John 13 above and in Paul's first letter to the Corinthians (1 Corinthians 13:4). This is what characterizes us as followers of Jesus and causes others to notice what a difference Christ makes in our lives.

I recently came across an interview with the longest-married couple in the world, Herbert and Zelmyra Fischer, from North Carolina in the United States. They had been married for eighty-five years. Here are Zelmyra's thoughts on what makes a good marriage: 'Marriage is not a contest; never keep a score. God has put the two of you on the same team to win . . . We are individuals but accomplish more together.'[9]

Zelmyra has drawn attention to one of the obstacles to becoming an effective parenting team. There is no room for contest or keeping a score. But how difficult it is *not* to keep score of who is 'working harder', 'getting less sleep' or 'contributing more' when it comes to sharing the parental load! Why do we feel the need to keep a running tally of who has put in more hours at the office, changed more nappies, cooked more meals? Almost all parents seem to slip into an unhealthy habit of comparison and competition with each other in an attempt to prove their worth and to justify who most deserves a rest. If we want our families to be a place from which mission can flow, then we need to do whatever we can to become a brilliant parenting team, and this means working together effectively.

This forms the basis of our joint mission and discipling of our children. Discipling them means modelling and teaching how to live wholeheartedly as a disciple of Jesus, and equipping them to grow in their relationship with God. We may not agree as a couple how this should be done. We may see eye to eye on subjects like Bible stories and family worship, but not on how to discipline or whether to let our baby cry in his cot for longer than ten minutes. Some of our differences in style can come from the way we ourselves were parented. As Nikki, mum to Joel, eleven, and Cameron, seven, says: 'It can be hard if you have a different approach to parenting and different childhood issues from your spouse. In those initial days you have to find a way to work together as "mum and dad". It is especially tricky for me as my parents divorced and I had quite a lot of negative childhood experiences.'

It takes time and patience to explore the conflicts we face as we set out to parent together, especially if those conflicts are based on pain we experienced in our own families. Can we begin to speak honestly about our expectations of parenting and what lies behind our assumptions and preferences? Is there a way we can come to a joint decision on the most important aspects of how to parent and disciple our children?

Another aspect of effective teamwork is juggling each partner's needs and the challenges of work or church alongside the care of the children. Conflict can arise when one partner feels their needs are not being met or their gifts are not being used.

When Azariah and I found ourselves repeatedly having the same arguments about who was doing what around the house and who was going to look after the children, we were encouraged by a friend to do a 'needs and time' audit. First we had to write down what we felt our greatest needs were. For example: sex, child-free time, time to watch films, a glass of red wine at the end of the day. Next we described how we spent our time in an average week, dividing it up into different sections (such as work, leisure, kids). We then had to discuss these with each other and with our friend.

Not only did this reveal surprises about our needs, but it was fascinating to see how our time was really being spent. If one of my primary needs was 'time alone to be creative', and I was looking after the children all week, it explained why I often escaped upstairs as soon as Azariah came home from work, thrusting a couple of small children into his arms! Our mission as a family will often be linked to our needs. I know someone who is brought to life by telling people about Jesus, and her husband supported her 'need' by helping with the crèche for the Alpha group at her daughter's nursery. I love this example of teamwork!

What are your individual needs as a couple? How can you work as an effective parent-team to meet these needs? Does one partner need to make some sacrifices to fulfil the other's needs? How can we create marriages which are characterized by mutual sacrifice, support and humility, so that each partner can flourish and our teamwork can demonstrate Christ to others?

Here are two parents who share how they work this out. Ruth, mum to Zoe, four, and Phoebe, two, talks here about the impact of her husband's support on her ministry: 'My work involves evenings, weekends and out of hours. Without my husband Ron and his support and view of ministry and family, I wouldn't be able to do this. He's so proud of me and believes in me and my gifts and calling. The impact of what I do on him is massive. Ron makes the juggling possible and is 200% committed.'

James, dad to Evie, five, Tess, three, and Seb, seven months, said:

My role as dad is about thinking of my wife and my kids before myself. All too often it seems as though marriage and kids are thought about from an individual's rights or own needs first. I don't see it like this and therefore I choose to live my life in a way that actually brings greater freedom and rest and enjoyment through putting my family first. To me, putting others first isn't being soft or letting others walk all over you. It is actually true strength. Often, putting someone else first becomes a two-way street. For my children to see this in action makes me feel they are getting the tools they need to live on this earth, learn, understand and become who they want to be.

These parents are saying that the key to an effective parenting team is loving each other with a Christ-like love (John 13:34–35). Our marriages can only bear missional fruit if we love each other as Christ has loved us.

In parenting we have to remain constantly flexible. What works one week won't work the next, which is why we need the wisdom of the Holy Spirit.

Praying together is a key way of strengthening our roots in God, and receiving his help through the Holy Spirit. Many couples feel uncomfortable praying together, or have never got into a regular habit of doing so. But praying with our partner for our marriage and for the people in our lives is a powerful act of unity. And it doesn't have to mean long hours spent on your knees. Azariah and I like to pray just before going to bed: sometimes these prayers are short and quickly followed by the sound of snoring!

Other couples we know read Bible notes together to nurture their faith, sing worship songs in their lounge, prayer walk in the countryside or respond to an inspiring Christian podcast. Our marriages need to be safe places where we can lovingly challenge each other to become more Christ-like, confess our sins and encourage each other to use our spiritual gifts. Seeking God together as a couple makes our family a stronger base from which mission can flow.

Marriages with deep roots in Christ's love and which nurture friendship, intimacy and teamwork will bear fruit in three areas. Firstly, marriages like this will strengthen us as individuals and as a couple to live out the callings God has for us instead of being constantly drained. Secondly, our marriages will model to our children what kingdom life is like, and will give them a secure base from which to live out their callings. Thirdly, our marriages will demonstrate, to those around us, something about the nature of God. Marriages like this are signs of God's coming kingdom. They point to Jesus and who he is.

Are your twin trees rooted in God and bearing fruit? Seeing my marriage as a mission team in which our aim is to work together, pooling our gifts, championing each other's vocations and parenting the next generation together, is an exciting perspective. We are part of God's bigger team, his church, which is slowly yet beautifully revealing more of his light and life to the world. Let's commit to seeing our marriages transformed so that God's love and grace can flow through us to others.

Questions for exploration

1. In what ways has your relationship with your husband changed since having children? How are you responding to these changes?
2. Find some time this week to talk with your husband about some of the issues raised in this chapter. What one thing can you do now to nurture friendship, intimacy or teamwork?
3. Reflect on your marriage as a foundation for missional living. In what ways is God using your marriage to love and bless those around you?

TALES FROM THE FRONTLINE

Anna

(mum to Josiah, seven, Esther, five, and Samuel, three)

Anna and her husband Rich head up 3dm UK (www.3dmuk.com), an organization that works in Europe and Australasia coaching churches and church leaders to be disciples, helping them to create a culture of discipleship and mission in their lives, ministries and churches.

I grew up in a Christian home, and made a commitment to faith when I was sixteen. After university, I did a gap year in India. I loved being there, and observed many different people living out their faith passionately, not just in words but through their lifestyle as well. When Rich and I got married, we went back to India to test whether we felt called there together. We discerned that it was a 'no' at that time, but I felt the Lord say, 'Why wait to be a missionary?' We came back to Sheffield knowing that there was a massive harvest here and that we needed to take responsibility to live as missionaries in the city. We had a heart for the poor and felt it was right to move to the inner city.

So when Josiah was born we were already living in a poorer inner-city area. We effectively became cross-cultural missionaries. I was aware from the outset that wherever I went I was different from the people I lived among. This was the context I became a mother in and this was my reality at toddler groups and in the community. I found that having a baby gave me so many more opportunities to connect with people, and I loved that.

When we moved to another inner-city area with people from our church, I joined a team who had established regular patterns of community service, including door-knocking. I wanted to be involved in all that the team did, so I would do this with Josiah, who was mobile by then. It was great, but I knew that my missional approach had to change when one day we were praying for a woman with a bad leg, and I couldn't pray because Josiah was whacking the washing machine with her crutches. I began to see that mission couldn't just be about events or activities. For me, it needed to be about relationship, and those relationships needed to reflect my season of life (recognizing that I was no longer a young adult with no kids!). I was called to share Jesus with people in a more incarnational way, living everyday life among them and with them, rather than just doing something 'for' them.

Our home was in the centre of the community and we began to open up the house and our family to those around us. That was when we saw most fruit. We got to know one particular lady that the team had already met, who was a drug user and prostitute. One day, she walked past our house in tears just as we were heading out to buy a Christmas tree. I chatted to her, and invited her along to buy the tree. She came back home with us and helped set the tree up, and it marked the start of a great relationship. She began to come to our house every day at 5pm. She would arrive, put the kettle on, often bringing her own biscuits, and just help me with the kids. It became a place of security and family for her. We would pray with her and read the Bible together, with our eldest joining in. I instinctively knew this was the best way for God to use me in mission – through building relationships in a home that was easily accessible to people.

What we said to her, and what we say to others, is 'You're welcome to come round at any point, and we'll tell you if we're not able to see you', so that the onus is on us to make the call, and people know they are welcome. Learning how to rest when there are lots of people in your house has been a challenge for me, as has opening the door when the house is a mess or you feel vulnerable. But this is all part of discipling people through our life, not just from our best side or best performance!

There have been times when living as a family on mission has been really difficult, but we've always learned from it, and gained more than we've ever given.

3. CHARACTER: GOD IN OUR BROKENNESS
By Joy

Guard your heart above all else, for it determines the course of your life.
(Proverbs 4:23 NLT)

When I was fourteen, I was preoccupied by boys, fashion and music, roughly in that order. I always had a strong faith, but in my early teens these other interests took priority. I was dragged along to a weekend away with a church youth group, protesting how uncool this would make me look, and while there, I encountered God and recommitted my life to him.

Overnight I went from teen fashionista to teen evangelist. Socially, this was not a good move. I was neither sensitive nor moderate in my evangelistic approach. My friends were not impressed. At that time, I thought sharing information about the good news of the message of Jesus was all I needed to do. It never occurred to me that the way I shared this message mattered.

In my twenties, with small children, I found that I fell into the trap of thinking my life needed to be attractive and successful in order for people to be interested in the gospel. I put more time and energy into looking competent in the outside world, and less into dealing with whatever might have been festering inside me.

Through a period of soul-searching, I realized that I am, and will always be, a work in progress. I came to understand, through my stumbling attempts at evangelism, that while sharing information about the gospel is needed, sharing the reality of your life and faith with others really makes a difference. I began to let people see my doubts, my questions, my struggles and my pain. I allowed friendships to deepen even though (shock, horror) those friends would see that I was a less than perfect Christian with a less than perfect life.

As we reach out to others in mission, it's easy to think that we can only be effective when things are going well. Most of us will have had that play date when our child snatched toys, blew raspberries and ran around naked (no? maybe that's just me) and we lost our cool. But this doesn't mean that our friends won't encounter God at work in our lives. As one mum explains: 'God has taught me that he uses me as an imperfect mother with disobedient children. I have realized that people aren't necessarily drawn to Jesus only if I have quietness to talk and my children are perfectly behaved. I can see that God uses my and my children's muck, and that it's his power that changes lives, not mine' (Satarupa, mum to Dinah, six, and Leo, four).

It can be easy to think that mission is all about sharing a perfectly packaged message, but we worry that if people see our mess, they may not see Jesus. We need to realize that the 'message' is in the 'mess'. God is at work in the midst of our imperfection.

In this chapter, we're going to be thinking about what is going on in our own hearts, in the knowledge that God values the reality of our lives, is at work in us and chooses to share his love through us.

A 'good' mother?

I recently watched a documentary about what it means to be a good mother. The presenter interviewed six very different mums with clearly defined philosophies of mothering. One was a real risk-taker, who took her toddler around London on the front of her bike with no helmet. Another was a home-schooler with seven children. There was a mother who was planning to breastfeed and share a bed with her daughter for as long as she wanted, and another who worked thirteen-hour days and kept up with her toddler through video calls.[10]

A quick online search yields thousands of parenting strategies for any confused mum needing friendly advice. We've all had that moment of panic, when our toddler hasn't slept for what seems like a lifetime and we hit Google. The advice might range from letting them cry it out every night for a week, to taking them into the marital bed until the onset of puberty. Since time began, parents have been faced with conflicting tides of opinion about how to raise their offspring.

But what if parenting is not about developing a toolkit of strategies and best practice that will enable us to weather the storm? What if the quality of our parenting is fundamentally governed by the state of our own hearts?

I've been a mum for a while. I've worked with kids in churches, schools and a mental health clinic, and this is what I've noticed: kids are, by and large, incredibly resilient and accepting. They come to love their parents as people in their own right. They don't care about prevailing parenting fashions, and roll their eyes and forgive freely our fads that see us on a 'clean the universe' mission one week and tripping over trainers in a bid to get to the front door the next. As I watched the documentary I couldn't help thinking that, as long as they were loved and cherished by their parents, each of the children would probably develop into fine, well-balanced adults despite their parents' bizarre parenting styles.

We are broken
Many children live in complex blended-family situations, manage transitions of life such as school and house moves, and cope admirably well with sickness and bereavement. Life is different for all of us, and some families experience more than their fair share of pain and difficulty. This is because we live in a broken world, and we ourselves are broken parents raising broken children. Our brokenness manifests itself in many different

forms: pain, fear, anxiety, insecurity, habits and addictions. It may be the result of things that we have done, or things that others have done to us. Whatever the back story (and we all have one), living as a broken person in a broken world is painful. Could it be that while our brokenness remains unacknowledged it poses a bigger challenge to our children than we realize?

Avoiding pain is time-consuming and costly. Will we try to buy our way out of despair, filling our lives with possessions? Will we feed our physical appetites when we feel starved of love? Some anaesthetize themselves with work or compulsive exercise; others keep people at arm's length because loving another carries risks of loss and rejection.

Whichever of these strategies we ourselves use most, following Jesus as we try to make sense of life in this broken world changes everything. In him are promises of life, fullness, wholeness and redemption for all of creation (John 10:10; Romans 8:18–28; Ephesians 3:18–21; Colossians 2:9–10; 1 Timothy 2:6). While our pain and brokenness may seem to define us, we have to learn to square this with the knowledge that he has 'disarmed the powers and authorities [and] made a public spectacle of them, triumphing over them by the cross' (Colossians 2:15).

The challenge then, is this: will our lives be defined by our attempt to outrun our unresolved brokenness? Will we continually find ourselves trapped in cycles of behaviour that are intended to help us avoid our pain at all costs? Or will we resolve to live in a way that entrusts our brokenness to the only one who can really deal with it, so that we can be freed to live in the promise of his love and extend it to those we meet?

This really matters. It matters because God has great plans and purposes for our lives (Jeremiah 29:11). It matters because 'It is for freedom that Christ has set us free' (Galatians 5:1). It matters because living a life that demonstrates God's love to others is incredibly hard to do if your own heart is a battleground.

Our children can deal well enough with our mistakes and quirks. But how might they deal with parents whose denial of their own brokenness leads them to pass it on, to repeat their parents' mistakes?

So where do we begin?

We love our children; we want to shape these growing lives in the best way we know how. They come to us as a unique package of personality and potential, and we come to them with a multi-layered woven tapestry of experience, family history, personality, spirituality, gifting, life circumstances and relationships. For good or for ill, their lives will be woven into and shaped by our own story.

We all have so much to give to our children. And we are all so broken.

We all remember our child's first major injury, don't we? I have three boys, so I could take my pick with stories to tell at this point – we have had football injuries, climbing frame accidents, bike incidents, stick-battles gone wrong, one impaling, head-bumps and knee scrapes galore – but I remember vividly the first time Isaac, my eldest, hurt himself badly. He was almost two, it was teatime on a summer's day, and I was heavily pregnant. He was playing happily with a friend when he tripped, and cut his forehead open on the corner of a coffee table. There was a sharp intake of breath, and then the scream. Then a totally disproportionate amount of blood.

We parcelled up our firstborn and drove in a panic to the hospital, where he bounced and played while I sweated with heat exhaustion and anxiety. He was patched up, and we returned home with our 'broken' boy. It healed, but it seemed that every time he fell over for the next six years he landed on that scar! We call it his 'Harry Potter' scar.

Many of us carry injuries like Isaac's: old wounds that have been reopened again and again. These wounds might have come from stinging words or bitter memories. Broken relationships, tattered dreams, empty promises, our own behaviour and that of other people . . . the list goes on. These are places where scar tissue has become part of who we are, holding healthy and damaged flesh together.

What does it mean to have a calloused heart?

In Matthew 13, Jesus uses the words of Isaiah to explain why some of his listeners could not grasp hold of the offer to participate in the kingdom of God that he was presenting to them:

> This people's heart has become calloused;
> > they hardly hear with their ears,
> > and they have closed their eyes.
> Otherwise they might see with their eyes,
> > hear with their ears,
> > understand with their hearts
> > and turn, and I would heal them.
> (Matthew 13:15 [Isaiah 6:9–10])

The dictionary definition of 'calloused' is 'unfeeling, insensitive or hardened'.[11] We develop calluses on our skin when they are repeatedly exposed to friction. When this occurs, that area of skin becomes less sensitive, deadened.

In Jesus' time, when nearly everyone worked manually, and walked in desert conditions in footwear that was not exactly made by Nike, hardened skin was normal. But a calloused heart? This is a heart that has become insensitive to not only its own pain, but also the pain of others. Calluses don't appear overnight. They are the result of processes that are habitual, reinforced again and again. They are the body's way of creating a defence so that the pain of the affected area can no longer be felt. I wonder if the process of our hearts becoming calloused works in a similar way?

A search of the number of biblical references to 'heart' yields 725 results. Clearly God takes the state of our hearts seriously. When Jesus quoted Isaiah (see the verse above), he was using an idea that was familiar to his Jewish listeners: the concept of a hardened heart. The Old Testament refers to this state on numerous occasions: in Exodus, Pharaoh's heart is hardened so that he consistently refuses to free his Israelite slaves; in the prophetic books the prophets yearn for the hearts of the people to soften and turn back to God.

I wonder what it is then and now that causes our hearts to become calloused and hardened in this way?

I wonder what the impact of a calloused heart is upon our capacity to parent our children and live missionally in the world?

We're going to explore two different ways that our hearts become hardened and less responsive to the Spirit of God. And we'll think through the impact this might have upon our lives, upon our relationships and upon our capacity to live with and for God.

These two areas can be broken down into two simple words: sin and pain.

There, I've said it. It's not nice and it's not pretty, but we need to talk about it, so make a cup of tea, brace yourself, and prepare to delve into shadowy places where none of us would go if we didn't need to.

Sin

Missing the mark, falling short of God's plan for us, just plain disobedience – these are all ways we can think about the word 'sin'. It's not a popular word, perhaps something that even as Christians we're embarrassed to talk about. Like the elephant in the room, we all know it's there, but we try not to talk about our own, and we certainly don't mention anyone else's (well, not to their face). There's no way round it – read the whole Bible: unresolved sin hardens hearts. Fact.

We can see in the biblical stories that failure to do what God has asked is a key factor in the hardening of our hearts. The story of the newly freed Israelite nation in Exodus is a classic example. They struggled to take God at his word; they grumbled at Moses and doubted that they would ever reach the Promised Land

(Exodus 16 – 40). Once there, after forty years of struggle in the desert, their courage failed at the thought of the armies they would need to face to secure their heritage. They were repeatedly drawn in by the charms of the new cultures that they encountered, and they began to worship a bizarre and diverse array of foreign gods.

How different is it, really, for us trying to follow God today?

How often do we struggle to take God at his word as we work out the complexities of family life?

How often do we doubt that God's promises for our lives will be fulfilled?

How often do we lack the courage to take on the battles for the heritage that God has for us?

How often are we enslaved by the lure of our culture and its trappings, only to realize that our lives look just the same as everyone else's?

I'm not saying this to take us all on a guilt trip. (I love that expression – I have a beautiful mental picture of a bunch of women with downcast shoulders climbing aboard an old and battered coach as I write. The guilt trip is a round trip. It will go nowhere, and it has no purpose, so climb off the bus, ladies! This is not our destination.)

I say this to bring us freedom.

The battle to believe what God has said in his Word and to our hearts is real. It is difficult to keep believing the promises held out in God's Word when everything that life throws at us shouts a different message. It is a challenge to stay focused on building a life that will take us to the places that God wants us to see and be part of. It takes focus and determination to refuse to be held hostage by the culture we inhabit, with its pretty things, its promise of happiness and its tireless pursuit of the next satisfaction.

Our God knows that following him is costly. Jesus himself described the challenge of following the 'narrow . . . road that leads to life' (Matthew 7:13). But here's the thing: it leads to *life*.

When we think of 'sin', we tend to think of the obvious things, but it's not all about 'sex, drugs and rock n' roll'. For many of us, the battle over our hearts is much more subtle: who did we judge today? What experiences are we hoping will fill the void we feel? Have we been still or are we relentlessly active in the pursuit of our own goals? This is just the roll-call of my sins from this morning. I could go on.

The sinful state of our hearts is a reality that we must all accept. Often, it is revealed to us most acutely in our closest relationships. Our selfish, snappy natures may be easy to mask in company, but are harder to hide in our own homes. In answer to the question 'What have your children taught you about yourself?' one mum responded, 'That I am sinful and find it very hard to love unconditionally!' (Satarupa, mum to Dinah, six, and Leo, four).

The Anglican prayer of confession explores the ways that sin can entice us: 'through ignorance, through weakness, through our own deliberate fault'.[12] I take comfort from knowing that sometimes when I lose my way it is a result of ignorance and weakness, but I have to acknowledge that there are also times when I am deliberately disobedient.

I have always had a weakness for shopping. I love clothes, and can easily convince myself that the top I want is really what I absolutely need. I am no stranger to that inner dialogue of personal justification at the checkout, but one day God helped me draw a line in the sand. I had gone out to buy a pair of practical work shoes, and I came home with a sparkly pair of silver kitten heels. They were a thing of beauty. They were also unnecessary, uncomfortable, utterly impractical and I couldn't afford them. I bought them anyway.

Don't misunderstand me. I'm all for the blessing of great shoes, but there was something else going on in my heart that day. It wasn't just about buying the shoes. It was a deeper compulsion. Vanity and greed were there and I wanted to satisfy my appetites with a quick placebo rather than actually bringing my needy soul into the presence of God. I wore them straight away – there was no going back.

That night, I had a vivid dream. I was wearing my pretty silver shoes, but there were heavy iron chains around them, and those chains were dragging me backwards, downwards, to who knows where. I woke up with conviction raging in my heart. I had known all along that I shouldn't have bought them. I looked at the shoes neatly packed in their box, and realized I would never be able to enjoy them, for they showed how my heart was ensnared by disobedience. There's nothing wrong in itself with buying sparkly silver shoes, but what *was* wrong was being a slave to my hunger for more, driven by my vanity. The sparkly silver shoes just weren't pretty any more. I know about grace and forgiveness, but those shoes had to go. I sold them on eBay, and was glad to see them go.

The problem is that when sin has a hold on us it creates an obstacle between us and God. It causes a blockage in our spiritual life. A place begins to develop in our hearts where we cannot reach out to God or feel our need of him, and that area becomes starved of the oxygen of his presence.

Even those of us who have been Christians for a long time can easily fall into the trap of trying to ignore these areas, sweeping them under the spiritual carpet and hoping they'll just disappear in a cloud of dust. Is this because we forget about the incredible power of God's grace and forgiveness? We think that we need to fix things ourselves and we get trapped in a cycle of guilt and shame. Fear, anxiety, unworthiness and self-loathing all conspire to keep us out of the arms of our heavenly Father – but this is where he longs for us to be, and when we are in his restorative presence it is impossible for our hearts to stay hard.

> For I will take you out of the nations; I will gather you from
> all the countries and bring you back into your own land. I will
> sprinkle clean water on you, and you will be clean; I will cleanse
> you from all your impurities and from all your idols. I will give

you a new heart and put a new spirit in you; I will remove from you your heart of stone and give you a heart of flesh. And I will put my Spirit in you and move you to follow my decrees and be careful to keep my laws. Then you will live in the land I gave your ancestors; you will be my people, and I will be your God.
(Ezekiel 36:24–28)

Can you hear the longing in God's voice here? Can you resist the God who promises to gather us, clean us, restore our spirits, recreate us and enable us to live with and for him?

The process of repentance is life-changing. We read in 1 John 1:8–9: 'If we claim to be without sin, we deceive ourselves and the truth is not in us. If we confess our sins, he is faithful and just and will forgive us our sins and purify us from all unrighteousness.' It was self-deception that got me to the point of buying my sparkly shoes, and when we are deceived, we can't see clearly what is in front of our faces. The reality is that, like my shoes, sin comes with a heavy price tag. It chains and ensnares us and costs us dearly because it estranges us from the heart of God. We're often trapped by our sin in the wasteland of guilt, but repentance brings us home. It removes the obstacles between us and God so that we can know his mercy, his faithfulness, his cleansing and forgiveness.

We need to know the power of forgiveness every day in family life, as one mum explains: 'In any family, forgiveness is key. I say sorry to all of my children and they say it to me. We're all in it together. We're all failing people so we all need to say sorry. When someone does something wrong, it is sorted out and then never mentioned again. You have to let go' (Esther, mum to seven grown-up children – three of her own and four adopted).

It is so easy to forget that it is God who takes the initiative in drawing his beloved people away from the places that have held them and hardened their hearts. Allow his love and forgiveness to sink into your soul and soften you today.

Pain

On my second birthday, as we were travelling on the motorway to my grandparents' house, my dad died at the wheel of our car. He had suffered from a heart condition all his life, but his death was sudden and utterly unexpected. The car crashed into a telegraph pole and flew into a field, flinging my mum and me out of the passenger door. Somehow, I emerged with only a few bumps and bruises. My mum's injuries were so acute that she was in hospital for almost a year. I lived with my nana (my dad's mum) and aunty (his sister) for that year. They were amazing Geordie women whom I loved wholeheartedly and whose uncomplicated generous spirits enabled them to parent a bereaved toddler in the midst of their own grief. I can only begin to imagine what they and my mum went through.

It's a story I can tell pretty concisely in a paragraph. I don't exactly dine out on this family history, but when I do share it I can see people's mouths widen and their faces sadden. At this point my defences kick in, and I try to protect myself and my audience, saying, 'I know it's really sad, but I'm used to sharing this – it's been the wallpaper to my life.'

'It's been the wallpaper to my life.'

I can't really think of another way of describing my story. My life has not been governed and defined by the sadness of what happened on that day, but it has irrevocably shaped me. It is my background.

That background includes pain and positives; strengths and weaknesses that are a part of me, forged in adversity and lived out every day. For example, I am strong. Too strong. A kind of 'nothing is going to take me down' defended and guarded strong, which God has needed to soothe and bypass with his gentle love again and again. That strength and resilience has sometimes kept me going and at other times kept people out.

I have also had to revisit my sadness and grief too many times to explain here, gaining different perspectives on a loss that has shaped me in every developmental stage – from being a small child to parenting my own small children.

These early experiences have been like a thread unravelling bit by bit. At times, knots formed that needed to be untied. Sometimes they were too tight and too complex for me to unravel alone, and at these times I had intense encounters with our heavenly Father that gave me a new perspective. Let me tell you about one of those times.

I was eighteen, and was at a Christian conference. I felt lonely and unsettled. I was doing a year out programme, my mum had just remarried, and I was living with strangers. Although I was having fun, and spending time with friends enjoying my new-found adult freedom, I felt rootless and disconnected. It was a time when my 'stay strong' mentality was fully in place, my defences high.

The people at the conference were really meeting with God. It was a pretty intense charismatic event. Nothing at all was happening to me. I felt nothing. At the last meeting, a woman was praying for me, and when nothing perceptible happened outwardly, I could sense her disappointment.

She went to get someone else, and brought a kind-looking older gentleman across. He prayed for me, and I can't remember a word he said, but this is what happened: I saw in my mind's eye a dark field. It was breezy, and there was long grass swaying. It felt like the middle of nowhere. Suddenly, I saw a small toddler in a summer's dress running through the field. The child was all alone, and terror and sadness instantly gripped me: this looked dangerous and wrong. I felt incredibly protective of the child, outraged at her situation. I thought to myself, 'This child needs help – someone needs to come and scoop her up, make her safe.' As I thought this, I heard the gentle voice of the Father saying, 'This was you after the accident, and all the emotions that you are feeling now is how I felt about you when you were in this situation.'

Getting the tiniest glimpse of the Father's heart for me in my darkest hour was transforming. Feeling his pain at my loss, and his desire to reach out and help me in the midst of it, began to melt my heart. Why did I need to work so hard at keeping myself strong and together when God in heaven felt so passionately about me? The experience was probably over in seconds, but its impact on my life has been immeasurable. It was a moment when my reality and God's heart collided. It changed me.

Every single one of us has a story. We have all experienced hurts and sadness, pain and loss. These wounds in our soul can be places where we encounter the love, grace and healing of our heavenly Father, and yet so often they remain places that are deadened and calloused, defended and inaccessible.

Have we any idea how much our God is longing to meet us in these broken places?

We're so frightened of the pain we think that encounter might cause, so concerned with what it might mean to let God into the wastelands of our hearts. We wonder how we might function without the defences we have built to protect our vulnerable places.

And yet when God reaches out to us and asks us to lay our pain before him, I have always found that his gentleness and compassion takes my breath away. The Bible tells us seven times that God is 'slow to anger and abounding in love' (Exodus 34:6; Numbers 14:18; Nehemiah 9:17; Psalm 86:15; Psalm 103:8; Joel 2:13; Jonah 4:2). How quick we can be in our own minds to reverse that verse and keep the love of our Father in heaven at arm's length!

Clearing the way
What does it mean, then, to allow God's presence to soften our hearts? This is not a simple journey by sat-nav. Often, it's much more like walking in the dark.

I want to walk with God with resolve and persistence, so that when I trip up on some sin and brokenness that I hadn't seen before, I won't let it block my path. Something that has really helped me on this road is a verse in Hosea:

Sow righteousness for yourselves,
  reap the fruit of unfailing love,
and break up your unploughed ground;
  for it is time to seek the LORD,
until he comes
  and showers his righteousness on you.
(Hosea 10:12)

There are four principles that we can dig out of this verse:

1. 'Sow righteousness'

This is about choosing what to invest ourselves in. Like a gardener carefully planting seedlings into the ground, it is an intentional action. When we make a conscious decision to sow righteousness, we invite God into our hearts more fully, because it is impossible to discern how to walk a righteous path without the ongoing guidance of the Holy Spirit. Trying to be a 'perfect Christian' will just bind us up in legalism and failure. Each of us is learning to walk with God, and looking for places in our own lives and the lives of those around us where we can share his goodness.

2. 'Reap the fruit of unfailing love'

This verse demonstrates the reality of God's covenant love. His commitment to us is that his love never fails, whatever our circumstances. As a response to God's incredible love, we his people try to live lives that sow righteousness in the world around us. As we do this, we hope that we will see fruitfulness. It might be tempting to take a simplistic view of this principle, and create a maxim for ourselves that if we live godly lives, nothing bad will ever happen to us. As most of our lives show, this is simply not the case.

While life may bring many ups and downs, God promises us a love that will not fail. This is a love that is with us on the mountain top, and carries us through the eye of the storm. It

takes real courage to hold on to these words when life is challenging. We have to remind ourselves that it is God's love that is
unfailing, not ours.

3. 'Break up your unploughed ground'

This verse is about dealing with our unresolved sin and pain. The
process goes like this: the first half of the verse, sowing and
reaping, talks about what is constant in our relationship with
God; this is what we do normally when the land is level. 'Breaking
up our unploughed ground' is what we do with terrain that is
unproductive. The rocks in the ground are all the things that we
talked about earlier: our pain, hard-heartedness, brokenness and
sin. So what practically can we do with these things?

One of the most crucial ways that we can work through our
'unploughed' areas is in community. Who are we walking with?
We all need people alongside us who can pray, offer accountability,
share childcare so we can get some headspace, and (importantly)
make us laugh. We need to regularly ask God for forgiveness,
especially when our journey has taken us way off the beaten track.
There may also be times when we need more help to unravel
some of the knots that are binding us. There is real wisdom in
seeking qualified professional support when it's needed.

4. 'Seek the Lord, until he comes'

It's dark, you've tripped over a rock on the ground and you're
flat on your face. You're hurting, you're tired, you feel shaken
from the fall. You know that you could pick yourself up, but just
as your five-year-old would wait for you to rush across when they
trip at the park, you also want to be scooped up, dusted down
and set back on your feet. Isn't this need for comfort and reassur-
ance a most basic human longing? God's Word tells us that he is
coming. It doesn't tell us when. It may be the hardest thing to
seek him when we're face down in the dust. Holding on to this
hope may use up the last of our reserves, and yet his coming
does not depend upon our capacity to seek. He is coming . . .

Wounded healers, mothers, missionaries

And it will be said:

'Build up, build up, prepare the road!
    Remove the obstacles out of the way of my people.'
For this is what the high and exalted One says –
    he who lives for ever, whose name is holy:
'I live in a high and holy place,
    but also with the one who is contrite and lowly in spirit,
to revive the spirit of the lowly
    and to revive the heart of the contrite.'
(Isaiah 57:14–15)

How I love these verses!

This chapter has unashamedly focused not on the outward roles of mother and missionary, but on our own internal state. For some of us, this is not comfortable reading. Many of us would much rather be 'out there', knee-deep in gritty reality, than reflecting upon our innermost emotions. But living as a missionary means bringing our whole self to God, so he can use us for the growth and spread of his kingdom. Mission is not just what we do. It is who we are.

We live in a culture that prizes capability, and many of us Christian women are highly capable. We juggle family life, career and ministry, and work hard to make much of this look effortless (ha!), but what if our capacity creates a stumbling block for ourselves and those around us?

This broken world does not need perfect Christians. Our children do not need perfect parents.

What God can really use is people with open, accessible hearts.

When our hearts have been softened and renewed by our heavenly Father, we will know what it is to live as wounded healers. This is what our broken world needs to see. We have been wounded, we can still feel our wounds, and yet we seek to share his healing love wherever we go. We resolve to address the brokenness in our own lives so that it will not be an obstacle for ourselves or anyone else. I love the picture of God's people clearing the path in this verse. When I read it I see teams of people with ropes pulling huge concrete blocks out of the middle of a highway. Isn't this a picture of how Christian community can be? Doesn't this show us how important it is to clear the path so that others, trapped in their own sin and pain, can see God? There is so much in each of our hearts that can get in the way of the incredible things that God longs to do in and through us. Let us resolve together to get the road ready. Many others need to walk this way with us.

Questions for exploration

1. Ask God to show you areas in your life where sin or pain is looming large. Can you think about how these areas might affect your parenthood, or your capacity for mission?
2. Can you identify any behaviour strategies that you have developed in order to avoid pain? What are their impact?
3. Are you aware of any places now where your heart has become calloused or hardened? Can you invite God's presence to soften these places?
4. The end of this chapter focuses upon removing the obstacles that keep us and others away from God's presence. How can you practically embark on this process? Who is walking this journey with you? What is the first step?

TALES FROM THE FRONTLINE

Marie-Christine
(mum to three children aged twenty-one, eight and five)

Marie-Christine is a survivor of the Rwandan genocide of 1994. She arrived in the UK in 1998 after seeking asylum in three other African countries without success. In 2001 she set up Safe Refuge Rwanda (www.saferefugerwanda.org) to support Rwandan refugees and victims of the genocide.

I survived the Rwandan genocide of 1994. I had to travel through four countries on the run with my young daughter. Sometimes we had nothing to eat for days and I had no idea what would happen to us. This is the story of so many Rwandans.

After four years of instability I finally settled in the UK. I didn't know which of my friends or family had survived. They were scattered all round the globe. I got a job which allowed me opportunities to travel freely within Europe, so I visited many Rwandan refugees who lived there. I mainly visited single mothers who had lost their husbands and/or children. Some had been raped. They had wounds caused by the loss of their loved ones, their culture and homes, and the abuse that many had been through.

This verse has been an encouragement to me: 'Praise be to the God and Father of our Lord Jesus Christ, the Father of compassion and the God of all comfort, who comforts us in all our troubles, so that we can comfort those in any trouble with the comfort we ourselves receive from God' (2 Corinthians 1:3–4).

I experienced the love of God which healed me and restored my dignity, giving me peace and hope. I believed that what God did for me he could also do for other refugees, if I was only available to reach them. I started to pray for them.

In November 2001 during my morning prayers I was in tears as I begged God to touch the body, mind and hearts of these refugee women that I had been meeting. I kept hearing a voice saying, 'Who can reach out to these women?' Then I sensed God asking me, 'Can you go for me?' It was a difficult decision to leave my job, but when I did, I had God's peace. It was my utmost pleasure to respond to God's call.

From that point on, I prayed and felt drawn to the presence of God. He began to reveal to me strategies to help these refugees. Firstly, he led me to do a course in mentoring and counselling refugees. I also did several theology courses and a Christian counselling course. Secondly, I started visiting refugees who were living in Europe, Canada and the USA, and invited them to stay with me; particularly lonely women or single parents who were depressed and could not cope with their daily lives. My mandate from God was to let them know that he cares for them. I would sit with them, talk to them, cook and clean for them, and take them to the local shops and churches. I became a voice in the churches and refugee communities for those who couldn't speak for themselves. I linked them up with others so they had support in their local communities.

In 2008 the Lord expanded my vision. He wanted me to also be a voice for survivors of the Rwandan genocide living in Africa. Their needs were different from those of the refugees in Europe. They lacked basic provision: shelter, food, clothes and medical treatment. I recently took clothes and money to Congo and Kenya to help mothers with small children. I know what it is to see your child hungry and not have any food to give. I also know what it is to hold a sick child with no possibility of medical care and to be watching closely to see if he or she gets better. When I arrived in the UK and had access to food and medical care, I made this vow to God: 'I will never keep money in a savings account while I know someone who doesn't have anything to feed her child.'

I had two more children after God called me to minister to refugees. My children are my main ministry. God knows that I am now a single mum. He knows my situation. God never tells us to forget our responsibilities. I do everything I do because his love is flowing through me. This is the kingdom of God. It's in my DNA. Sometimes I plan to go on a mission trip; then I feel my children need more of my attention, so I don't go. When they do come with me on these trips I make sure they go to parks and I spend time just sitting with them. I cook the food they like. I try to keep to our usual routine.

My dream is to help refugees rebuild their lives so they can help their children. It is very important to invest in a parent, especially a mother. You give your children what you have. They lack a lot when you don't have much to offer, because you can't draw water from an empty well. I am so happy when I think of some of the families I know who were striving to survive but now are thriving. They have got an education and jobs, and are happy. Their children are doing well at school or university.

I don't know the plans that God has for my own children. I just ask God to make me a faithful steward of them so they can be the people God wants them to be. I depend on God in everything because he has proved to be a loving, caring and faithful Father. I also pray that I will faithfully and fearfully be a good steward of my time, resources and abilities.

4. FOUNDATIONS: BUILDING A HOUSE, SHAPING A VILLAGE

By Joy

> *Your people will rebuild the ancient ruins*
> *and will raise up the age-old foundations;*
> *you will be called Repairer of Broken Walls,*
> *Restorer of Streets with Dwellings.*
> (Isaiah 58:12)

I love the image that this Bible verse creates in my mind. Whenever I read this passage, I see the same picture: a higgledy-piggledy street, with lots of different houses, all different ages, shapes and sizes. I imagine standing there and looking around – who built these houses? What are their stories? Whose lives have they sheltered?

It's a passage of Scripture that I have been drawn back to again and again. God has used these verses to speak powerfully to me about the call he places upon mums: to be builders and shapers of lives and communities that demonstrate his love. Surely this is at the heart of missional living?

As Christians in a secular age, our lives are open to observation and scrutiny from those who are exploring how our faith changes our lives. As one mum explains: 'Family and relatives who are not Christians are now watching us to see what it looks like when two Christians raise children. What does discipline look like? What does love look like? And what kind of kids does it result in?' (Ruth, mum to Zoe, four, and Phoebe, two).

In this chapter we're going to think about what kind of a life we are building in our families, and we'll consider some useful ways to build a family culture that is 'mission focused'. We'll draw on some biblical images of homes and house building, and think through what these might mean for us today.

We might sometimes describe our family as a 'household'. Could we imagine for a moment that our family is an actual house standing in a real-life community?

Let's think about this. It means that:

- we need foundations
- we have to be built
- others take part in our construction
- we will stand near other houses
- we will experience decay and disrepair
- we will change.

The Bible uses the imagery of building a house to explore the way that God's people shape their lives. In the book of Proverbs, the virtue of wisdom is characterized in the original Hebrew as a woman:

> Wisdom has built her house;
> she has hewn out its seven pillars . . .
> The fear of the LORD is the beginning of wisdom,
> and knowledge of the Holy One is understanding.
> (Proverbs 9:1, 10 NIV 1984)

The word 'hewn' implies effort. Serious work goes into the construction of a life that demonstrates wisdom and godliness. It requires hard graft: costly decisions, sacrificial choices, persistence, perseverance and determination in the face of opposition.

Or, looking elsewhere in Proverbs 14, we read: 'The wise woman builds her house, but with her own hands the foolish one tears hers down' (Proverbs 14:1).

There is a steady stream of choices available to us every day, covering every possible aspect of how to live our lives. My daily choices include deciding whether to get up when the alarm rings and spend a few minutes being resourced by my heavenly Father, or stick my head under the pillow and weep at the list of things to do. I know my own weaknesses. There are times when I ignore my bored toddler, sitting in front of the TV, in order to steal five minutes on Facebook. When the noise of bickering from upstairs rises over the cranking of the tumble drier, I have to think through whether to engage with the conflict between my pre-teens, or let them work through the complexities of their relationship by themselves. At my toddler group, I need to choose whether to reach out of my comfort zone to the lonely new mum, or stick with my friends. In all of this, the overriding question is: will my life decisions be driven by what I feel and want here and now, or by the principles that undergird the life that we as a family are working together to craft?

I have a friend who recently blogged about her family's decision to develop a 'family contract' together. This is what she says:

A friend of mine suggested we make some kind of family contract and I thought this would work brilliantly for us. I felt the Lord lead me to 1 Corinthians 13 – the obvious place to start, really. It's all about what love actually is. It's how God runs his family. I sat down with the family and we looked at the Bible passage, finding all the key words I'd printed off and laid out on the kitchen table, and we talked about what they meant. Then, I presented them with our framed 'Family Way of Life', which they loved, and we all signed the back, promising to 'live a life of love'.

(Kaitlyn, mum to Emma, eight, and Jessica, six)

For many of us, it could be an incredibly powerful exercise to make clear decisions about what our core family values and principles are going to be. We will all live out our deeply held beliefs, whether consciously or not. The process of deciding as a family how our value system is going to be shaped can bring a sense of purpose and freedom.

Recently, I've been thinking a lot about foundations. I've been drawn back time and time again to Jesus' profound teaching about the wise and foolish builders:

> Why do you call me, 'Lord, Lord,' and do not do what I say? As for everyone who comes to me and hears my words and puts them into practice, I will show you what they are like. They are like a man building a house, who dug down deep and laid the foundation on rock. When a flood came, the torrent struck that house but could not shake it, because it was well built. But the one who hears my words and does not put them into practice is like a man who built a house on the ground without a foundation. The moment the torrent struck that house, it collapsed and its destruction was complete.
> (Luke 6:46–49)

A few years ago, my husband and I fostered an eleven-year-old boy for two years. He was older than our children, who were then five and three. We were pretty clueless about eleven-year-olds, and although he was and is a lovely young man, fostering was tough. Early on, when we were getting to grips with some of our foster child's habits and behaviours, my husband Clynt said to me, 'The thing is, Joy, he's a house without foundations.' This simple comment spoke volumes to me. Of course, this isn't strictly true; eleven years of life and experience had formed him, but his 'house' was wobbly and unsafe. If he was to grow and thrive, he needed some serious underpinning.

Foundations and capacity

Something that is true for all of us is that we cannot build a bigger or stronger house than our foundations will allow. As Jesus, or a civil engineer will tell you, the building above the ground is dependent upon the building below the ground. Jesus tells us clearly in this passage that a well-built life is one that is founded upon both hearing and learning to live out his teachings.

We are all called by God to be and do different things. We may have a call to minister at the school gates, in the workplace, or on the other side of the world. Wherever we are called to be, our relationship with God is the cornerstone of who we are; all that we are able to do and be for him comes out of this. Nevertheless, there are seasons in our lives where we may find that we have more or less capacity to live out the mission that God has called us to. It is helpful to explore the link between our foundations and the capacity we have to live for God in the world. This image helps flesh this out:

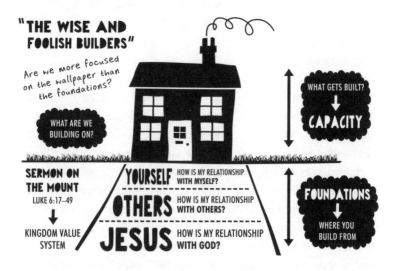

The story of 'The Wise and Foolish Builders' above was taken from Luke's Gospel, but it is also part of the Sermon on the

Mount, found in Matthew chapters 5 – 7. These passages contain Jesus' teaching on the value system of the kingdom of God. They come right at the beginning of his public ministry. We could see them as his manifesto; he is setting out his core values, explaining what a life that is defined by following him might look like.

If we break these teachings down, they fall into three basic categories:

- How we relate to God (Jesus)
- How we relate to others
- How we relate to ourselves

As I was growing up, I was regularly told that I was named 'Joy' so that each letter of my name would remind me that life functions best when our priorities are oriented around loving Jesus, others and yourself. My mum wisely told me that a life that works this way will know joy whatever else befalls.

When we are thinking about building a missional life as a family that is fixed upon sure foundations, this is where we need to begin.

I want us to explore how, practically, we can build up these three aspects of our foundations: our relationship with God, our relationships with others, and our relationship with ourselves.

Our capacity is what the world sees above the ground, but this is completely shaped and developed by what is happening below the ground. It always needs to be this way round. Our foundations are developed first. Our capacity can be built from there.

If our foundations aren't functioning well, we may still be able to build something that looks impressive, but the test of the life that we are shaping is what happens when the storm comes. As mums, it is all too easy to focus on building a life that looks great to onlookers – wings and turrets are all very well, but aren't much use if they collapse at the first gust of wind.

Relationship with God

Our ultimate foundation is our relationship with our Creator. This is where our identity is anchored. In him we find rest and purpose, healing and wholeness. It is from here we are sent out into the world to live a life of love. For all of us in this rat-race world, it is a challenge to remember that everything we are able to do comes out of our identity in God. If we never did anything for God or anyone else ever again for the rest of our lives, his love for us would not be altered. This is a mind-blowing thought. Nevertheless, for most of us, testing out this theological precept is hopefully not an option as we get busy in the world in a multiplicity of creative, diverse and inspiring ways.

It's a real challenge in the busy life of a mum to stay focused on our relationship with God. It can be easy to feel that having a 'quiet time' is just another job on the to-do list, another area where you may feel like a failure before you even start.

I find it really difficult to maintain a regular rhythm of using Bible-study notes, but for some people, these can be a lifesaver. Whatever method or system works best for us, our relationship with God must be built on the knowledge of his love and grace: our God's emotional currency is not guilt but love. God longs to meet with us and be a part of our normal daily life. Here are just some of the practices that I and some of my mum friends have found helpful as we invest in our relationships with God:

- **Setting reminders to pray on your phone:** In the busy daily grind, regular prayer can slip off the agenda. Using technology to set regular prayer times can really help. Anna and her family say the Lord's Prayer together at twelve noon and six in the evening. Once, Anna's phone beeped to remind her to pray while we were in the John Lewis footwear department. So we did. It was fun, slightly bonkers and holy all at once.
- **Devotional sites and emails:** Many Christian organizations write daily online devotional resources. If

you're a busy mum working in an office, what better way to begin the working day than with a cup of tea and a five-minute devotional at your desk? I use the daily texts sent out by the Moravians, but there are many other websites to choose from. (Please see the appendix for a list of useful devotional resources.)

- **Sermon podcasts:** Many churches put their teaching onto their websites. You could set aside time to listen to inspiring teaching, especially if looking after children in the evening or a permanent involvement in crèche in the morning is keeping you out of church services.

- **Reading the Bible with your children:** I've recently come across *The Jesus Storybook Bible*.[13] This is a fantastic resource for reading Bible stories with younger children, but it's powerful for adults too. I have regularly found myself welling up as a familiar story touches my heart in a new way.

- **Worship music in the car:** For those of us who find ourselves in the car alone, listening to worship music can be a great way to engage with God while on the go.

- **Twitter and blogs:** Twitter and other social networking sites can be fantastic places to hear stories and read blogs about what God is doing in other places. It has never been so easy to know what is happening around the world, and to be inspired, stretched and challenged as we read about other people's experiences and views.

- **Text prayer:** It is quick and easy to put together a text message that others can respond to. I have learned that when prayer texts arrive from friends, the easiest thing for me to do is to stop and pray there and then, asking God if there are some comforting words or a Bible verse that will speak to their situation.

- **Christian books:** Taking the time to read and invest in Christian books can grow and stretch your faith – could you read a book with some friends as a book group, and be challenged together?

- **Daytime Bible study with childcare:** Some churches run a daytime Bible study with a crèche so that stay-at-home parents have the opportunity to meet with God together. This is a great way to go deeper with God yourself, but is also a great way to draw people on the margins into Christian community. Is there a group like this in your area? Could you think of starting one with some friends?

- **Accountability groups:** Having one or two friends that you are accountable to, and meet with regularly to share encouragements and struggles, can be a great way to stay sharp in your faith while raising children. They can be a place of prayer, challenge and resourcing in even the most difficult situations.

- **Booking in solo retreat times:** Is there somewhere you can go to get away from it all and have some time with God, perhaps for a day or two away from the pressures of life, to quieten your soul? There are many retreat houses and conference centres throughout the UK that offer inexpensive and creative ways to spend time with God.

- **Lone coffees:** It is understood in our house that if I do a childless supermarket shop, there will be a solitary coffee involved afterwards. Sometimes it is important to stop and catch your breath, and to notice the sacred in the midst of the ordinary. An extra fifteen minutes to pause in the midst of the busyness to pray, reflect and be still can recharge and refresh us more than a caffeine hit.

- **Journal:** For some people, journaling can be an intimate way to connect with God. I have always found that the process of writing clarifies my thoughts and feelings like nothing else.

- **Have a cup of tea with Jesus:** There are times in life when maintaining any kind of devotional rhythm can feel like an uphill battle. When we hit these times, the temptation is to throw the towel in, but these are the times when we need to live in grace, not guilt. Just as we would sit down with a friend and have a cup of tea, we can have a cup of tea with Jesus. This is a time to stop, refocus and pour out the things that are weighing our hearts down.

I'm inspired by the story of Susannah Wesley. This eighteenth-century mother contended with more difficulties than most: she gave birth to nineteen children, nine of whom died in childhood. Her marriage was difficult, she home-educated her remaining ten children, and the family home burned down. She would regularly sit down and throw her apron over her head. This was a sign to her children not to disturb her, as she was praying, sometimes for up to two hours a day. Her sons John and Charles went on to lead the revival that began the Methodist movement.

God loves it when we draw close to him, and he always wants to welcome us into his presence. Can we begin to explore new ways to meet with God in the midst of our busy lives? This will fuel us for a life of mission.

Relationships with others

Understanding the impact of our relationships is crucial because they shape who we are. At best, they support and hold us, and at worst, they tear us down. We are all held in a complex web of relationships, with our husband, children, parents, in-laws, siblings, friends and colleagues. For some, this network is life-giving, a powerful springboard for loving and serving God and others. For others, much time and energy may be spent navigating through relational and emotional turmoil. Just one difficult relationship can have a massive impact upon our capacity in the rest of life.

Having children changes all our relationships. It may unearth beauty we hadn't seen before in a relationship. Conversely, it may challenge a relationship that had previously seemed solid and secure.

We may be so exhausted that we have less time for friends, even though we need them more than ever. We may feel our friends without children cannot understand what we're going through. Relationships with parents and in-laws can be an untold blessing, or cause additional stress – it's different for everybody. The one certainty is that we and our relationships will be changed.

I love these words from a mum about the pleasure she has found in seeing her own parents as grandparents: 'My relationship with my mum has grown closer as I can see the pain I put her through as I was growing up. Also, watching my parents interacting with my children is better than eating chocolate!' (Jennet, mum to Ben, eight, Archie, six, and Millie, four).

Our own capacity to parent our children is always going to be impacted by the parenting that we ourselves received. Many aspects of our parenting unconsciously re-live the messages hard-wired into our own souls as we grew up. If those messages were grace-filled and loving, they will equip and resource us well. If they were not, we may need to consciously explore the places where our working model is broken and needs adjustment. We might ask ourselves: what are we going to have to unlearn and relearn in order to parent in a way that will sow spiritual and emotional health, and good life habits into the hearts of our children? The challenge is not for us to strain to become a 'perfect parent' with 'perfect children' (can you imagine?), but it is about shaping a family life that will create a solid foundation that our children can build from. God has such incredible things planned for them and us to build. I often think about how we might live differently if we really had a sense of the destiny that God envisages for us, or our children or maybe even our great-great-grandchildren. What we create today will be the platform upon which future generations build.

How we relate to ourselves
How are you?

The interplay between your emotional health, physical health, spiritual health and life circumstances brings tremendous blessing or severe limitation, or a mixture of the two.

Shaping a life that functions well is a complex business. I am constantly trying to tweak and adjust our family life, to convert us from a rickety carriage of chaos into a smooth, well-oiled machine.

In my 'master-plan', I will turn out three well-mannered, well-educated, hygienic men of God. They will cook, clean, pick up their own underwear, and make sensitive, thoughtful husbands and fathers. They will serve powerfully in the church, make a difference in the world, pursue a range of sports in their spare time and will live comfortable, financially secure, happy lives into wizened old age. Clynt and I will look on from our dotage, nodding with pride and gleaming with a sense of accomplishment. For some reason, in this mental image, we are all American . . .

Reality check! I really hope that life is going to be great for my boys, but I already know that it will be a whole lot messier than my pipe-dream. God in his infinite grace does not need us or our lives to be perfect before he can use us powerfully. While I would love to see my children's lives unfold without pain or adversity, this is never the case for any of us. The challenge, then, is for us to build a life that is 'real-world proof' – where our wellbeing is not fundamentally dependent upon our outward circumstances, but where we are realistically aware of the impact that our circumstances have upon us. Each one of us is building a life amidst a hotch-potch of imperfection and complexity. Some of us are raising children while ill, or grieving. Some of us live with the daily grind of financial worries or difficult work situations. All of these circumstances, and myriad others, can have a huge impact on our wellbeing. In stressful times, our emotional and physical health can take a battering, and it's so important to recognize their impact on our overall capacity in life.

Just recently we were running an Alpha course. I had felt under the weather all day, and it was as if my whole life was playing catch-up with jobs left undone and pressures mounting.

As we prayed before the session, I said to God, 'I have nothing; so tonight, you can have my nothing.'

The topic was Prayer, and as we talked about answered prayers we discussed the difficulties one of the group members, Lucy, had been having a few weeks previously. I had prayed for each problem with her on that day. Twenty minutes later she had texted to say that one of the issues had been unexpectedly resolved. During Alpha, I reminded Lucy about this, and she said that on the same day her husband had come home with some money they had been owed that had been unexpectedly returned – another answer.

Then an older lady, Pearl, told her story: last summer she was very ill with a lung condition. My husband had visited her. Pearl explained that, when he prayed, she had felt an unusual warmth going through her body. From that point on, her health had improved. We had no idea until the Alpha session that this had happened! We could now explain to Pearl that the healing she had received had come from God.

I began that evening feeling defeated and exhausted, but by the end of the session I was energized, ready to discover where else God was busy at work! Our 'nothing' is all that our Creator God needs. His everything is more than enough.

One, integrated life

We can put such pressure on ourselves to be amazing, to be competent and to hold it all together.

God's perspective on this is life-giving. Colossians 1:17 explains: '*In him* all things hold together' (my emphasis).

We don't have to have it all worked out, sewn up and put together for ourselves. The foundation of our lives is 'the rock that is higher than I' (Psalm 61:2). He holds all things together in our crazy lives. The stumbling blocks in life can seem insurmountable to us. The way forward is to entrust both our nothing and our everything to our heavenly Father.

Life as a mum brings many challenges. How do we shape an

integrated life? In our busy culture, we can develop a tendency to try to control our environment by compartmentalizing. In our minds, we try to separate our commitments into the 'work' box, the 'home' box, and the 'church' box. What would it mean if we made the decision to build a life that is all in one box? If we focus on building a life where we make decisions based on our vision, values and principles, rather than on our circumstances? This is by no means a simple quick fix.

In 2008, I got the job of my dreams, working full-time as a trainee Child and Adolescent Psychotherapist in an NHS clinic. Our children were nine and seven, and I had worked for three years to get the necessary qualifications. Clynt had also just completed his ministry training, so we were both ready to embark on exciting and different new careers. As soon as I began my new job, I discovered completely out of the blue that I was pregnant with our third baby. While this was an amazing blessing, it put a significant kink in our well-made plans. My job was in a different city, with long hours and extra study. How on earth could we manage a new baby and two new careers alongside the two children we already had?

It felt as though God had drawn a line in the sand. Our lives were not going to follow the trajectory we had so carefully plotted. There were big decisions to be made about our new life. After much prayer, counsel and soul-searching, we ultimately made the decision that I would leave paid work in order to support the family, develop mission work alongside Clynt, and write this book. This decision was born out of the realization that we as a family have just one life. We wanted to make sure that our life was integrated, that we were a team with one goal, rather than individuals being pulled many different ways.

Pursuing an integrated life will look different in each season of our family's life. But it is the sort of life where we can be responsive to the call of God, the needs of a child, a pressured work deadline, or a need in our community, because we have thought through what is possible for us all together, and we have built a life that is proactively seeking to live out deeply held principles, rather than reactively seeking just to get through each day.

Building your family culture on a solid foundation

I can be a real people-watcher, and I love to observe the 'cultures' of different families. There are families who are super clean and organized – everything is pressed and ironed, the house immaculate and the lawn beautifully stripy. Then there are families who are a hotch-potch of chaos and disorder. I had a friend who lost a pet hamster in a piano – he was never seen again. We all know families where this is possible! There are serious families, silly families, academic families and practical families, outdoorsy families and indoor families – I could go on. We are all different, and each of us as parents will bring different strengths and weaknesses into the melting pot of the family identity that we are shaping. What are the key elements of your family identity? What are the core beliefs, values and preferences shaping your family culture? What traditions are you creating that express it?

In our family, the children know that Friday night is sacred time for Mum and Dad. It is the only night of the week when the children eat separately from us. They might have friends to sleep over or watch a DVD while Clynt and I have a nice meal with wine. During the rest of the week, eating all together is a priority, time to share our 'highs and lows', listening to each other.

Over the years, I have been continually inspired by the creative ways that families have shaped customs and traditions around their core beliefs. What are your family's special rituals? It could be that Dad takes a different child out for Saturday breakfast each week, or that Mum takes each child to a café so that everyone gets one-to-one time. I know families who sing together in a regular music time and families who experiment with regular creative devotional times. As we learn to develop mission in the context of family life, we will be drawn into all manner of varied pursuits! For many families, mealtimes are an ideal opportunity to invite others to share in your life together. Developing a family mission culture might mean inviting someone to live in your home, or simply investing in a young person who babysits on 'date nights'. We might choose to create particular traditions around festivals and particular times of the year.

Last year when Isaac turned thirteen we invited significant men in his life, many Christians and some not, to participate in a 'coming of age' evening for him. In a heady haze of testosterone, my boy ate curry, drank weak shandy, and listened as men who have known and loved him from infancy shared their tall tales and wise words. It was an evening steeped in fun, deeply spiritual, and full of important moments that we hope Isaac will remember.

Something that has become really precious in our family is the New Year review of the year. We began this when our eldest boys were about five and seven. We sit with the boys over a great meal (takeaway curry is the current dish of choice). We talk through our highs and lows, and think about our hopes for the year ahead. We listen to music that has been significant for us in the year gone by, and look at a montage of photos of our time together. I am always surprised by the powerful memories these pictures evoke, even of those times when we felt that we were just plodding through life and getting by.

When the meal is cleared away and the memories have been shared, everyone else leaves the room, and I create our family 'word of the year' on the table, spelled out with tea lights. The boys come back in, get to read the illuminated word for the first time, and then I explain how we've discerned that this is the word we will reflect on and be challenged by in the days, weeks and months ahead.

This blending of the ordinary and the extraordinary is what family life is all about: a powerful mixture of chaos and order, poetry and nonsense, beauty and mess. What traditions will best express your own family's personality?

Becoming a family on mission

We have the opportunity to make conscious choices as parents about what our family is going to value, invest in and become. These choices will become part of our children's family heritage that they in turn will pass on to their children. What an enormous privilege and opportunity! Whatever else we are or do in life, we will never have a greater opportunity to influence and shape the lives of others. When thinking about the inheritance that we will leave behind, we must surely realize that raising children with a deep love for and relationship with God is one of the most missional activities we could possibly engage in: our kids and theirs after them will continue to be the hands and feet of God on this earth long after we have gone.

If you want to think about a long-term, world-changing mission strategy, it is simply this: shape a family culture that will clear the obstacles to spiritual and emotional development from your children's paths. Build a solid, sure foundation for your family on the Word of God, and then trust God with the rest. We can never guarantee that our children will be Christians when they're older but we can certainly make decisions now that can have a great impact on their spirituality.

This is exciting, but hugely challenging. We may not always feel that we, on our own, have all the resources that we need to invest in our families. The New Testament concept of household, known by the Greek word *Oikos*, doesn't relate well to our twenty-first-century concept of nuclear family life. Households in New Testament times would have been multi-generational, including parents, grandparents, aunts and uncles, distant relatives passing through and household staff. Children would have been raised with all these different influences. Various family members would have contributed something to the family melting pot, so that everything wasn't just dependent on the poor, pressured, beleaguered parents. As Amy Orr-Ewing, mum of three, explains,

As mums we get depressed, we feel guilty. We need to remember it's about the extended family, the Oikos household, not just about our nuclear family. No-one was meant to live just in a nuclear family like we do in the west. We are meant to live in a generous way, in community, which is positive for our children. We are meant to look after each other's kids and live as single people, married people and families with kids, all together.

Many of us may not have our biological extended family close at hand, but who has God put into our spiritual community? Who are the like-minded missionaries that we are committed to walking with? In this age of increasingly fragmented and broken families, it's a liberating challenge to explore who we might partner with so that we can enlarge our capacity to bear the load. In our family, we have often had other people living with us. At times, this has meant free babysitters (yeehah!). Other times, it has meant that I could take my boys to an after-school activity and return to a fully cooked meal. In return, we had the opportunity to share our home and family life with someone in the midst of a painful and difficult situation. Since I left paid work in order to give time to growing and shaping mission work on a local housing estate, people in our 'Oikos' have given financially in order to make this possible.

The challenges and pressures on family life are immense, and surmounting these requires creative thinking and innovation by an 'Oikos' that is committed to being on mission together. If we are prepared to live this way, the challenges may not feel so overwhelming, as we know that our little insular family isn't in this alone. We can draw on the resources of others who are journeying with us.

At the beginning of this chapter, we looked at a verse from Isaiah 58. This chapter presents a call to a radical lifestyle of mission: to defend the most vulnerable; to feed the poor and clothe the hungry. In doing so, Isaiah explains, God's people get to participate in the very architecture of the kingdom of God.

This is a truly incredible calling. We serve a God who is a master builder, and we get to participate in building his kingdom right here and now.

We build foundations, we build homes, we build lives, we build communities; we change the world.

Questions for exploration

1. Where are the places where your foundations need to be strengthened?

   - In your relationship with God?
   - In your relationships with others?
   - In your relationship with yourself?

2. The story of the Wise and Foolish Builders is all about hearing God's words and putting them into practice. What do you discern God saying to you and your family now? What practical steps can you take to begin to live this out?

3. What traditions, values, habits and practices best define your family culture? Think about these, write them down, treasure them – how do they enable your family to draw closer to God? What might you add?

4. Does your family culture enable God's love to be shared outside your family? What are some of the ways that you do this together? How could you begin to share God's love as a family more?

TALES FROM THE FRONTLINE

Hannah
(mum to Wilf, eight, and Amos, five)

Four years ago, alongside others from her church, Hannah set up 'Baby Basics' (www.kingscentreonline.com/baby-basics), a project that gives out essential equipment to vulnerable mums and their babies, specifically mums who are seeking asylum or who have been the victims of trafficking in the sex industry. Midwives, family nurses and health visitors can make referrals to the project, and the families then receive a Moses basket that is packed with blankets, sleepsuits, sanitary products and nappies.

Baby Basics began because the midwife for displaced people groups who came to our church was really moved by a particular little boy that she met. The little boy was two or three and his mum was thirty-seven weeks pregnant. They'd just moved up from London and it was snowing, and this little boy didn't have any shoes or a coat – he just had trousers and a T-shirt. Even though the midwife was used to seeing lots of people in lots of different circumstances, there was something about this boy that particularly touched her, and she said that she was haunted by his face when she went to sleep. She came to some mums at church, and asked if there were any clothes that they might have that were spare. As the conversation developed, the midwife shared the kind of situation that her clients were living in. We sorted out some clothes for that particular family and then we pulled together a group of people to think through what could be done about this desperate need.

We realized that we didn't know what was happening even just a few streets away from where we lived. Our children have so much, and there were people with so little – it felt shameful really. But we hadn't known.

We wanted to do something and didn't really know how. We had an American lady in our group who shared that, in the USA, church groups often pack school bags with school supplies for needy children. Someone said it would be great if we could pack a Moses basket with baby supplies because that would be big enough for everything we wanted to put in and it would also provide a bed. We agreed to do that to start with, but didn't think we could sustain it.

There was one time when we were given a basket as a donation, but it had no mattress in it, and this really bothered me – I don't know why. But I got very anxious, and tearful, crying over this stupid Moses basket that didn't have a mattress. I felt overwhelmed, like I shouldn't be even trying to do this project, like it was all beyond me. Later on I went to see a friend, and she walked into the room carrying a brand-new mattress for a Moses basket. 'Can you use this?' she said. 'I've just found it.' It helped me to realize that what we need will be there, that God will provide. I know that, as long as the stuff keeps coming in, I'll just keep doing it.

One day, after the first few baskets had gone out, I went to a wedding and we sang a song that has the line 'Break my heart for what breaks yours', and I just remember singing it and thinking, 'For the first time, I'm singing this and meaning it.' I think this is what Baby Basics is all about: our hearts being broken for the things that grieve God. It's singing that song and meaning it, and then being prepared to do something about it.

Some of these women don't even have sanitary towels to use, and that's not good enough. We can give things that will make a difference and help remove some of the stress from the first few weeks. I remember the enormous gratitude of one young mum; she was so grateful that someone had cared enough to give her shower gel to use after the birth of her baby.

One of the midwives some time ago phoned us up to say that she had just dropped off a basket to a family, and when she went back to the house afterwards, the house felt different. It might seem that all we give is a basket, some sleepsuits and a few nappies, but it carries something else with it. We pray over the baskets. The midwife knew that something had changed in the house even though she wasn't a Christian.

One day, we received a large donation and I was looking at the heap of stuff that needed sorting through. It was a hideous mess that I had to wade into and organize, and I felt grumpy and ungrateful and didn't want to do it; but then I had a picture of the presence of God over all those bits and pieces waiting to be used.

Baby Basics was three years old in March (2012). The first basket was collected on Amos's first birthday, during his birthday party, so it has grown up with my children. Last year we gave out 114 baskets and 90 other items. Members of another church, in Northampton, have just begun their own Baby Basics.

I'm grateful to be a part of Baby Basics, and grateful for what God has shown and taught me through it. I'm keen to keep going, to keep being part of something that connects our middle-class church to the people that Jesus would be hanging out with. Ultimately, I hope that what we do speaks eloquently of God's love and the love of his people.

5. STEPPING OUT: MISSION-MINDED MUMS

By Anna

> *[Jesus] told them, 'The harvest is plentiful, but the workers are few. Ask the Lord of the harvest, therefore, to send out workers into his harvest field.'*
> (Luke 10:2)

It was a swelteringly hot day in August and I was squashed in a hot bus with my eight-month-old daughter, Eliana. Surprisingly, Eliana sat contentedly on my lap grinning at the lady next to me. The lady smiled back, which elicited another smile from Eliana. This interplay carried on for a while as I chuckled and enjoyed the distraction from the heat. After a few minutes I decided to break the ice: 'Do you have children?' 'Ah, yes, I do,' she responded. 'I have five, but they're all grown up now and sometimes I wish they were still your daughter's age.' The lady told me her name was Dawn and we continued the conversation as if we'd known each other for years.

Dawn and I began talking about what a shock it is to have your first child; all the challenges of night-feeding, working out what their cries mean, no free time. The conversation led on to birth stories. I found myself explaining the intricacies of Eliana's birth to this complete stranger. I recounted how my legs had been in stirrups and that being sewn up afterwards had been the most excruciating experience of my life. After sharing these horrors, revealing I was a Christian and married to a vicar didn't seem a big deal! Dawn began asking why we had chosen to lead a church on a housing estate and had made the choices we had. Soon she and I were in deep conversation about church, faith and life – all thanks to the engaging smiles of an eight-month-old.

My children often open up opportunities for me to start conversations. They have no inhibitions, and their wide-eyed trouser-tugging often elicits a response. By being themselves, they create a chance to connect, empathize, care for and laugh with people. I have found that having children bonds you with other mums very quickly. A shared language and understanding often exists between mums, and provides an amazing opportunity to build relationships.

We may not realize it or feel it, but as mums we are in a unique position. Not only are we ideally placed for missional living, but we are perfectly equipped by God to be his 'sent ones' in his world and to live as disciples of Jesus. Right now, right where we are, whatever we feel like, however many hours we are working, we can live out our God-given callings and connect relationally with those whom God has placed around us. We don't need to wait for a 'better time', when we will have fewer interruptions and more energy. We can be used by God just as we are.

As we explored in chapter 1, we are all 'sent ones', sent to go into the world and make disciples. And so are our children. 'Going' may look different with children. We may not feel we are 'doing' anything 'missional'. Perhaps we feel guilty about this – guilty that we are only just surviving as mums, never mind getting 'out there' and making an impact in the world.

But the challenge is this: no matter what our circumstances, do we have a mission mindset in everything we do? Are we willingly offering our whole lives to God, so that our words and actions point towards Jesus – our time, money, choices, speech, emotions, shopping habits, eating habits, TV-watching, internet usage? And are we encouraging our families to do the same? Can we think about our whole family being on, and involved in, mission rather than being tempted to split our lives up into several separate compartments such as work, leisure, and church, some of which involve God and some of which don't?

'Here I am, Lord, send me'[14] – but how do we know where to go?

A few months before Azariah and I were due to move to London to start his curacy (trainee vicarship) at a large, well-established church, we got a phone call. There was an opportunity for Azariah to lead a small church, St Francis, on a housing estate, which currently had six members and had been without a paid leader for two years. It would be a very unusual training post. As soon as we heard about St Francis we were excited, but nervous about the mission opportunities. Some of those involved in the 7/7 London bombings had been found on the estates where we would be based. There were high levels of unemployment and mental illness. It wouldn't be an easy ride. What should we do?

The choices we make as a family about where we focus our mission will have far-reaching effects not only on us as parents but on our children too. Often they will be counter-cultural choices which some of our friends do not understand. Our mission focus may be an area, a specific people group, workplace or a school. It may involve an activity: a sport, photography, craft, blogging, fundraising or philanthropy. It may involve a lifestyle: living in community, itinerant living or living without a secure salary. Our mission focus may call for tough decisions. We may move house, job, city or country, make sacrificial financial choices, or do things which, in the short term, are pretty inconvenient. They may affect which church we commit to. They will almost certainly affect how others perceive and speak about us.

I was intensely excited about the potential of leading a small church on a housing estate. In my early twenties I had begun praying about doing this kind of work at some point in the future. But Eliana was five months old and I wasn't sure about the effect this would have on her. If we stayed on the estate as she grew up, what would her peer group be? She would miss out on the high-quality children's work at the larger church where we would originally have been based. And how would Azariah handle the pastoral load of this church? Would we ever see him? It was a risky venture.

Starting with prayer

We needed to hear God's perspective. We prayed about it together. It certainly seemed that working on the estate would fit with what we felt passionately about– for the lonely to be in families (Psalm 68:6), for the rights of the poor to be upheld (Jeremiah 22:16) and for the marginalized to be included in God's church. Considering the opportunity in the light of our passions, gifts and circumstances, we got prayerful advice from close friends. We had a deep sense of peace about the decision and decided to say 'yes', even though we had many unanswered questions and knew it wouldn't be easy.

When we begin to see the needs around us, praying about our mission focus as a family must be the starting place. By listening to the still, small voice of God we get a sense of where he wants us to channel our energies. God's perspective on your situation may be that you need to step out of your comfort zone or it may be that you don't need to change anything – perhaps he is simply asking you to keep doing what you're doing. Or perhaps he is asking you to be a friend to someone, or to continue praying for your friend who is not a Christian. In Ephesians 4:11 we are reminded of the many gifts that members of Christ's body have been given so that we are equipped for works of service. These diverse gifts are to be used in love so that we can all work together as one body, each part doing its own work (v. 16). We all have different gifts. Some of us are evangelists; others are teachers or pastors. Some of us love details; some of us love the big picture. Our God-given gifts will imbue our mission with definition and intentionality. They will provide clues to the flavour of our mission as a family.

What is the one thing that you can intentionally do to use your gifts? Perhaps your mission focus is about using your home to be hospitable to others – for example, to welcome university students or teenage mums? Perhaps you have been blessed with money and can use it to support a charity? Or you could use your practical skills to help others mend their washing machine or put up their flat-pack furniture?

Saying 'yes' to a mission focus that complements our family's giftings will mean that we must say 'no' to another focus. This can be hard for those of us who want to do everything! I would love to get involved in volunteering for my friend's incredible charity '28TooMany' (some of you may be able to get involved, so check out the appendix for more information) which seeks to eradicate the harmful practice of female genital mutilation. But with the other missional things I am involved in, this will have to wait. We need to make choices that give us healthy boundaries. One healthy boundary could be volunteering for only one ministry at church in order to concentrate your energies on friendships in the community. If you struggle with these kinds of boundaries then speaking and praying with another Christian can clarify what God is calling you to right now. Healthy boundaries give us the best chance of loving our neighbour as God intended.

Loving our neighbour

'"Love the Lord your God with all your heart and with all your soul and with all your mind." This is the first and greatest commandment. And the second is like it: "Love your neighbour as yourself"' (Matthew 22:37–39).

When we arrived at St Francis I desperately wanted to make new friends. I decided that taking eight-month-old Eliana to a healthy eating and cooking class at the Community Centre on the estate would be a good start. Each week a group of about six of us were taught by Mandy, a dynamic NHS-employee, about the hows and whys of healthy cooking. We would all then prepare and cook a meal together before sitting to eat as a group. There was a crèche provided for the children. I loved the group, and Eliana was welcomed and included. I particularly liked Mandy, who made us laugh and was passionate about healthy food. I felt able to be myself in this context, without having a missional 'agenda'. Right at the end of the course, Mandy told me that she had heard I was the new vicar's wife and she was interested in coming to church occasionally with her three young children. We swapped numbers and continued the relationship. I began to pray for Mandy and her family and to get to know her better. Nearly three years on, Mandy and her three children are active members of St Francis. She is a gifted and inspiring single mum and her whole family are an incredible blessing to our church and family. God was already at work in her life and it wasn't anything extraordinary that I did that got her involved. I was simply there, involved in the community, being myself, able to encourage what God was already doing.

What I have learned through this is that the harvest is plentiful, just as this chapter's opening verse, Luke 10:2, says. Mission isn't necessarily about bringing people to activities at church. That is one way that God chooses to draw them into relationship with himself. Mission must be about loving our neighbour. If we, as mums of young ones, can meet people on their turf, ready to love, listen and pray, we can see not just individuals changed but whole families and communities transformed. God is calling us to be a loving presence in our communities and workplaces; to be ready, to be prayerful, to listen to the Spirit's promptings.

Listening to the Spirit is what Naomi, mum to Cayden, nine, Ben, seven, Eron, five, Noah, three, and Reuben, one, does as she chooses to love her neighbours through small acts of kindness:

I have learned that if you have a fleeting thought to do something for someone, always act on it, otherwise it's gone. It's really important for building friendship. A lot of my friendships have been based on this and have involved me getting out of my comfort zone. I knew someone who had lost a baby early on. She was not a Christian and I didn't know her very well. I bought her a bunch of white flowers which felt a bit like I was stepping beyond the boundaries. 'What will she think of me?' I thought. I left them on her doorstep and she was really touched. We've become really good friends since.

Friendship often springs out of the love we show to others when we are prompted by the Spirit – the kind words, the thoughtful gifts, the listening ear – but sometimes it seems like our seeds are just being thrown out to the birds. Sometimes we pray for opportunities to share Jesus with our friends and the opportunities never seem to come along. I have often found myself feeling discouraged, thinking, 'Am I just not bold enough about sharing Jesus?'

Being patient

'I planted the seed, Apollos watered it, but God has been making it grow' (1 Corinthians 3:6).

I have found it incredibly hard to make friends with mums on the estate. It's not for want of trying. In my first year of moving to St Francis I would arrive at one of the local Children's Centres with Eliana, often with my friend Gaby and her son, and look desperately around for someone to talk to. Even though Eliana enjoyed playing, some weeks I would come home feeling utterly defeated because I hadn't had a meaningful conversation with anyone. Was it worth going? Even if I did meet someone who I connected with, I often wouldn't see them for weeks, or perhaps never again! Making relationships wasn't happening quickly and conversations about Jesus were rare. Was I seeing people as projects? Was my 'agenda' scaring people off?

Here's what Gaby, mum to Jemimah, four, Joey, two, and Caleb, six months, said about the opportunities she has for sharing Jesus:

Opportunities don't come every day. One day there might be lots of opportunities. Other days there may be none. I actively seek opportunities to pray for people in day-to-day situations. Recently there was a woman at one of the Children's Centres who was really struggling. She was working full time and in the evening looking after her grandchildren as her daughter was unable to and she didn't want them to go into care. In my head I tried to work out all sorts of crazy schemes to help her, but I also prayed for her and told her so. When I saw her next, she was like a different woman because she had got a car. It was making her life so much easier. None of my schemes involved a car, but God knew what she needed and I believe my prayer helped in that!

Like Gaby, I have also found that opportunities don't come every day, and when they do, offering prayer, simple encouragement or a personal story of how my faith has helped me is a way in which I can plant seeds and water them, as 1 Corinthians 3:6 says. About two years after we'd moved to St Francis, a few opportunities all came at once over a few months. I had an opportunity to pray for someone's healing, a mum from the estate opened up to me, and another mum who I had met in the park and become friends with started asking me about how she could pray with her son at bedtimes and what Bible she could read to him.

My impatient self is slowly realizing that it takes time to build friendships, to plant seeds and to water them. Only God makes these seeds grow. People take time to get to know and trust us. We need to be honest with them about our own lives if we want them to be honest with us. This is the same whether we meet people in the community, at work or online. I have learned that sometimes it is simply about being present and ready, having the courage to speak about Jesus when we can (1 Peter 3:15–16), loving people without judging them, and trusting that God is already at work in their lives. Perhaps right now some of us need to trust God that friendships we have had for years *will* bear fruit, whatever that may look like, and that the prayers we have prayed faithfully have not fallen on deaf ears.

It can be disappointing when a mum friend moves away before we feel we've really had a chance to speak to her about God. It can be tough when an issue we're passionate about, like buying Fairtrade products or supporting homeless people, doesn't seem to be taken seriously by people around us. This is the stuff of life. And God is in the midst of it.

Can we trust that God is still at work in those situations and in people's lives? That even among the interruptions, missed opportunities and the waiting, we are part of God's bigger picture, playing a vital role as workers in his harvest field and being shaped by that, right where we are?

Mission and children: an interesting cocktail

It is challenging when my children are terribly behaved with the other children of a mum I am getting alongside. I have felt in the past that they have mucked up an opportunity. But God has taught me that he uses me as an imperfect mother with imperfect children. People aren't necessarily drawn to Jesus only if I can talk to them without interruptions and my children are perfectly behaved. I have learned that God uses our 'muck' and that it's his power that changes lives, not mine.
(Satarupa, mum to Dinah, six, and Leo, four)

As Satarupa illustrates, sometimes it feels that our children are obstacles in mission rather than being channels for mission themselves as in my opening story. How do we cope with that feeling of being between two roles – perhaps talking to someone about God at the school gates, while trying to stop our child hitting another child? Or wanting to attend the evening course where we are making good friends, but knowing that our school-age son doesn't want us to leave him with a babysitter?

Having children means that we are constantly interrupted and our plans can change at the last minute. It is encouraging to remember that Jesus was also continually interrupted in his ministry. Jesus was at a wedding in Cana when his mother interrupted him to say, 'They have no more wine' (John 2:3). Jesus responds by turning water into wine. In Mark 6:30 Jesus and his apostles are trying to get some peace and quiet. When they land on the shore, the crowds have followed them. Jesus' response is to have 'compassion on them, because they were like sheep without a shepherd' (v. 34) and he feeds all five thousand of them with five loaves and two fish. In Mark 5:21–43 Jesus is on his way to heal Jairus's daughter and is interrupted by a woman who is haemorrhaging. Jesus heals both the woman and the girl.

What can we learn from the interrupted ministry of Jesus? Could it be that the interruptions we face from our children are not obstacles or distractions at all, but God-given opportunities to love and sacrifice, to experience more of God's grace? Could our children be challenging our individualistic attitude towards our faith and ministry? What if we began to see our children as ways in which God can teach us about himself and how his kingdom works? Can we take his command to welcome them seriously (Luke 18:16)? What if we start to see ourselves as partnering with them in mission instead?

I had to figure this out when it came to the music-based toddler group Minibeats, which my friend Gaby and I started at church for the mums on the estate. Most weeks I could be found attempting to jump like a monkey or chug along to the wheels on the bus while balancing two-year-old Eliana on my hip and placating my snotty one-year-old son with rice cakes mid song. It felt as if I was trying, and failing, to do two jobs: welcome mums and care for my children. Conversations were often cut short by a spilt drink, a dirty nappy or needing to encourage my daughter to share toys. It was draining.

Perhaps it's not at a toddler group where you experience this frustration. Maybe you feel you cannot attempt to talk to strangers about God, when your energy is totally taken up with the basic needs of your children. Or you have an important meeting at work which will move a project you've been praying about for ages forward, but you have to bail out to go to your child's nativity play. There are all kinds of situations where we feel that our children are getting in the way of what we feel God has called us to do. And we feel guilty for feeling that way.

One turning point came for me during a quiet moment at home when my daughter announced, 'I work for Minibeats church.' This stunned me. Eliana said she worked for Minibeats. She felt she was involved in making a contribution to the group: perhaps by giving out instruments, playing with other children and entering into the activities herself? It struck me that Gaby and I weren't there on our own, but we were working with our children in mission.

Maybe this was part of what being a family on mission was about. Our children are also 'sent ones', learning to be little missionaries in their playgroups, nurseries and schools. I began to see myself as partnering with Eliana as a 'sent one' at the toddler group. We were working together to love and welcome people.

Here's how some other mums have developed ways to live missionally alongside their children.

Celia, mum of three, is part of a weekly 'Adventure Fridays' group which is a community of mums and their children who meet up every Friday to go to farms, parks and soft play areas and to build relationships with each other. Anyone new that they meet is invited to join in.

Sara, mum to Caleb, four, Seth, two, and Hannah, nine months, has started a choir called 'Hoxton Singing Mums', which meets on a Monday morning at her church with preschool children in tow. The children play with the toys while the mums sing anything from pop and gospel numbers to show tunes and Disney classics.

Naomi, mum to five young boys, helps to run a community called 'Make Space' which has run craft workshops for children and young people in her community. Two of her five children have joined in, along with other parents and children. She is doing something she loves, her kids are having fun, and she has seen how it has built confidence, friendship and hope in those who are involved.

I have learned that changing my expectations of what mission can be with young children makes all the difference. We *will* be interrupted. We will have our plans thwarted. We will miss out on conversations and meetings, but we will also experience the blessing of our child's perspective on a situation. Our self-centredness can be challenged by our children, our inadequacies exposed. Can we also see 'interruptions' as opportunities to teach our children what it means to be followers of Jesus? Anna Robinson, mum of three, in her blog (annarobbo.wordpress.com) talks about precious moments during the worship songs at church when she explains what the words mean to her daughter and realizes what a wonderful opportunity this 'interruption' is to disciple her little one.

Sometimes, we will have to stop certain activities for a season in order to prioritize our children's needs. For Gaby and me, pausing Minibeats for one term until our older children were at nursery was a good decision. When we restarted, we each had only one child to look after, there was a new team of helpers, and the pause had created an increased appetite from mums for the group. My children had been a channel in which God had taught me about the limits of what I could do – they had been a channel of grace. As we do mission together, we are teaching our children something of what it means to serve God and serve others.

Mentoring and discipling
'Therefore go and make disciples of all nations, baptising them in the name of the Father and of the Son and of the Holy Spirit' (Matthew 28:19).

Mission and discipleship go together. Jesus has called us not just to be 'sent ones' but also to make disciples. Disciples are learners, followers of Jesus, who want to spread his message. We are called not just to seek converts but to train them in the ways of God so that they too can train others. We do that by living our lives alongside people, exhibiting Christ's love, not just through our words but through our whole lives.

One way in which Lizzie, mum to Caleb, four, and Joseph, two, found to disciple others was to mentor a young person 'on the go'.

> There's a girl we've known since she was eleven. She is very vulnerable and has a lot of issues. She's nineteen now and she comes on and off to church. Something I can do now is invite her to come and hang out with me and the kids and do whatever we're doing. She doesn't have a job so she's available in the day. I can invite her round for tea, to come shopping with us or go to the park. She can 'do life' with us, see how we live and we can chat.

Who could you invite to simply 'hang out' with you and your children, maybe on a Saturday morning while you're doing your normal family activities? We can't overestimate the value of this kind of investment of time into someone's life, what it can teach them about Jesus as well as what our own children can learn from that person. I remember feeling really loved, when I was a child, by a couple called Steve and Linda from church who seemed to enjoy hanging out with me and my brothers. As I grew up and they had children, I enjoyed babysitting for them and still remember noticing things about their family that I wanted to emulate: their fun-loving attitude, enjoyment of games and their welcoming home.

Our God-given little disciples

When it comes to discipling others, our main focus has to be on our children, our God-given little disciples, equipping them for life as Jesus-followers. This is mission. Our children primarily learn from us, as parents, how to live in the way God wants in the world he has created. As Gaby, mum of three, says, 'Discipleship is not an injection. You can't make it in a factory. It's something your children have to see in the way you live and behave.' If we want to disciple them we have to allow ourselves to be discipled too. We can only pass on what we ourselves have learned.

Ruth, mum to Isla, six, Carys, three, and Keira, two, says this: 'Being a mum is my calling now and for the rest of my life. So Jesus is discipling me to fulfil that role, and wherever he leads me and whatever he teaches me will help me to be a better mother. My three children are my first mission priority.'

Discipling children will be different depending on their ages and temperaments, and on the character and nature of our family.

Caz, mum to Grace, four, Finn, three, and Elliot, six months, talks about the 'normality' of discipling her children:

> Every day is an opportunity to teach my children about Jesus, to demonstrate his love, to pray for people we encounter, to seek to grow in the fruit of the Spirit, to encourage them to pray for God to do more than we could ask or imagine, to worship together . . . When we see an ambulance, we pray for Jesus' healing power to come. Children are so interested and excited by Jesus, and our adventures with him are a part of normal life.

We can be creative as we model to our children what following Jesus means. What will they learn when we encourage them to invite someone with no friends at school to their birthday party? Or to write their teacher a thank-you note? Or to be a good listener? And what are the things that we can learn from them?

Anna, mum to Elijah, five, and Josh, one, was struck by her son's generosity and took it as an opportunity to grow in faith:

> Recently I told my eldest son what the harvest offering at church was for, and he went to get his piggy bank and give the majority of the

contents to the offering, £7.40 – a lot for a five-year-old. I wanted to say, 'Don't give that much!' But then I want him to develop joyful giving, which he has. It made me realize he doesn't have any worries about whether there will be food on the table or if the house will be warm. He knows his parents will take care of that. It made me realize that needs to be my attitude towards my heavenly Dad and his provision for my life.

Whether we realize it or not, the choices we make, the way we speak to people, who we invite (or don't invite) into our homes, how we spend our money and treat the environment – our whole lives are shaping our children. This can feel like a huge pressure but it needn't be. Jesus doesn't require perfection from us to do this job. He wants us to trust him, love him and, when we fail, to say sorry, get up and start again. He takes what we have and who we are and weaves it into his story of redemption. We can never guarantee that our children will follow Jesus later in life. If they don't, we don't need to blame ourselves. We just need to keep praying and trusting God.

My mother-in-law, Elvira, died in 2013 at the age of seventy-nine. She was a single mum, and had lived a life of faithful, prayerful devotion to Jesus. Her Bible was the most well-thumbed, thoroughly annotated Bible I've ever seen. She would excitedly share stories of God's goodness with anyone who would listen. Elvira prayed daily for her son, trusted God to provide for her, gave sacrificially to others, and was known for her playfulness and beautiful singing. Elvira played her part in God's story well, and hundreds of people attended her funeral. Her legacy also lives on in her son, who is spending his life in Christian ministry and who demonstrates in his own family and community the investments made by a passionate, missional mother. Elvira loved those around her, loved her son and, even though life was often tough, she kept going.

And that is what we are also called to do: to keep going, with our hearts open to his Spirit, loving our neighbour, loving our children and, even when we've missed opportunities or acted like idiots, to wake up the next morning and start again. This prayer is a great way to start: 'Lord, use me right where I am, here and now, just as you've made me, to love my family, love my neighbour and to do what you've called me to do today. Amen.'

Where are you right now? What gifts has God given you and your family? Who has he made you to be? That's where mission starts. It starts with ordinary acts of love which flow from who you are and who God has created your family to be. There are infinite possibilities and flavours of mission. We're all included in God's big story of redemption, whether we are focusing on individuals, projects, the home or the workplace. It's time to start the adventure and see the world transformed through ordinary, yet extraordinary, acts of love.

Questions for exploration

1. What opportunities has God currently given you for mission where you are?
2. In what areas or relationships is God calling you to develop patience? Carve out time this week to bring those areas to God in prayer.
3. How are your children involved in mission with you or how might they be in future? In what ways are you a 'family on mission'?

TALES FROM THE FRONTLINE

Danielle

(mum to Zion, ten, Judah, two, and Moses, four months)

Danielle Strickland is a Salvation Army officer who lives in Canada. She is internationally recognized as a leader, speaker, writer, justice advocate, mission developer, worship leader and church planter.

I think that living missionally means using your whole life as an example of God's kingdom come. This includes where you live, what you do, how you raise your kids and who is included in your family. We often have people living with us – so that naturally extends our community.

I think men are crucial in helping mums see their full potential. My husband spurs me on. He's hopelessly in love with Jesus and he wants me to do my very best towards this mission of ours to win the world for Jesus. He is a disciplined man with prayer, so his example is helpful.

I have learned a few things along the way that have helped me in my ministry and family life tremendously. One of them is that I don't have to do everything and that I must prioritize God's values. What he wants me to do must come first. God values the weak, the lost and the broken. We pretend we value this as well but actually we want to be strong, confident and pretty. We need to let go of the world's definition of 'success' and embrace a kingdom mindset.

I also think it's important to pursue meaningful relationships. This is the key to world-changing behaviour. God's kingdom always comes through relationships, and these can work best with family. I don't want to compartmentalize my life into sections but to use every part of my life to nurture relationships that are about God's kingdom coming. I have learned so much from the relationships in my life.

I've learned to appreciate the chaos in life and to let some things go, but also to cherish the things that matter. Sometimes we have cereal for supper as a family if we haven't had a chance to cook, we go to the park with the kids and talk to someone from our neighbourhood, or I simply 'waste some time' with the Lord just because he's worth it and it's the most valuable thing I possess.

Doing something together as a family can help so much: just doing the one thing that is in front of you. Your family might be able to host a Fairtrade chocolate party or get people to sign some petitions for a campaign. Perhaps you could do a 5 km run together to raise money for a good cause or do respite care for foster kids.

My greatest challenges are time restraints and fatigue. Often you feel pulled in different directions. Navigating those demands with the pull in the right direction at the right time is perhaps the greatest challenge. But I've learned that things can wait. God's kingdom isn't going to stand still because I don't have time to do something.

6. SURRENDER: WONDER WOMAN MUST DIE

By Anna

> *Going a little farther, [Jesus] fell with his face to the ground and prayed, 'My Father, if it is possible, may this cup be taken from me. Yet not as I will, but as you will.'*
> (Matthew 26:39)

The rise of Missional Wonder Woman

I have a favourite mug. Azariah gave it to me on my twenty-seventh birthday. It provokes comment every time I hand it to a guest. It shows a buxom superheroine with shapely thighs and a tight, red, white and gold 1970s all-in-one in several powerful, feminine poses, wielding her lasso of truth and indestructible bracelets which repel missiles. This Amazonian warrior princess, Wonder Woman, is known for her special powers of superhuman strength, flight, speed, stamina and agility. Wonder Woman and I have a lot in common, including the thighs.

My Wonder Woman mug signifies my love of the strength and resilience of our incredible female race and my desire to live uncompromisingly and authentically as a godly woman of influence. I long to use the gifts God has given me to their fullest extent and to be a cheerleader for other women wanting to do the same. That is the dream which inspired the book you are reading.

But I have a confession. When I began writing this book, my idea of what a missional mum looked like was Wonder Woman, soaring around the planet rescuing troubled souls, kids in tow, changing bag slung over one shoulder, cape flying, wearing a freshly applied coat of sheer red lipstick. That was who I aspired to be. I had picked up the idea that mums who could 'do it all' and 'have it all' (running projects, groups, volunteering, baking, preparing endless creative activities for toddlers, earning money, having regular deep conversations about God with strangers) were the ones who were truly bathing in the glory of God's favour and obeying the Great Commission in Matthew 28.

When I began writing this book we had moved to a new city. I had a newborn and a toddler to look after, no childcare, and was trying to support my newly ordained husband as he led a small church on a housing estate which brought with it all the intensity and uncertainties of starting a church from scratch.

I swiftly began my life as Wonder Woman, starting up and running the women's ministry, helping with the children's work, launching and co-leading a music toddler group, running a parenting course, a church photography project and, of course, trying (and spectacularly failing) to write this book, alongside the full-time job of caring for my small children.

I told myself, 'Mission is so important, isn't it?' If I didn't run the toddler group, who would? The parenting course was vital too.

I tried to ignore the nagging feeling at the back of my mind that, actually, with all the projects I was running, I simply didn't have the energy to dedicate myself to the most precious relationships God had given me: my children and husband – let alone the two mums in the community that God had given me a particularly strong connection with.

Clinging on

I tried to boost myself with spiritual half-truths, saying, 'Azariah and I have been called to the most challenging of urban ministries. It is expected that things will be difficult. Hasn't God called us to a life of sacrifice and perseverance?' and 'Doesn't Jesus command in Luke 9:23 that we should deny ourselves, pick up our cross daily and follow him?'

I regularly exploded at Azariah in rage over small things like shrinking one of Eliana's dresses in the wash. I would fall to pieces if one of the children didn't have their afternoon nap. My mission activities were sapping me, I wasn't allowing God to restore and refuel me, and I had no capacity to deal with the ebb and flow of life. My body and mind were hungry for rest. I longed to respond to the words of God in Isaiah 55:1–2 (NIV1984):

> Come, all you who are thirsty,
>   come to the waters . . .
> listen to me, and eat what is good,
>   and your soul will delight in the richest of fare.

In public I got used to the comments people made: 'I really admire you, Anna. You're amazing' and 'You are such an inspiration. You are one of the most organized people I know.' These words were a balm to my weary soul, the pat on the back that I craved, but also a heavy burden on my shoulders, an extra pressure to be the missional 'Wonder Woman'.

When friends tried to warn me away from all I was doing in order to concentrate on the children, pride would kick in. 'You don't know me,' I fumed to myself. 'You don't know what a high capacity I have. God has called me to mission. I am not wasting my potential.'

Crisis point

The crisis came one Thursday when Azariah was away overnight. Eleven-month-old Micah had got up at 5am the previous two mornings and was teething. Having put him to bed at 7pm, I was ready to turn in at 9pm. As I was sliding under the sheets he began to cry. Two hours later he was inconsolable. By 11pm his blood-curdling screams were scaring me and no amount of milk, rocking or medicine could relieve him. Unable to reach Azariah on the phone for moral support after seven attempts, aching with tiredness and feeling like I was reaching the edge, I came face to face with my desperate and un-surrendered self.

I didn't have Wonder Woman's lasso of truth or indestructible bracelets to help me out. I was not the super-achieving missional mum who headed up ministries. I was a helpless, panicked mess. My prayers felt like silent screams to a distant God.

When I finally got through to Azariah he persuaded me to call local friends for practical help. Finally, my mum came to the rescue, giving me rational advice on the phone and then driving two hours through the night to assist with Micah as well as two-year-old Eliana, whom he had woken up.

This situation wasn't about a crying baby and toddler or a string of bad nights. It was a crisis moment. A call to relinquish control of my life to my heavenly Father. We all have difficult nights and times of feeling helpless. This is part of being a mother. But sometimes the intensity and regularity of those feelings points to something deeper that God wants to heal in order to free us to become the people we were created to be: 'Come, all you who are thirsty, come to the waters . . .'

I realized that I was empty and had nothing. I realized that I needed to surrender to God and listen to his plans for my life. Micah's screams that night echoed my pain. My son did what I couldn't do – express my desperate needs and my dependency on others. God was beckoning me away from a life of fear and self-sufficiency and calling me to a new way of living that would form the foundation of true mission.

I surrender

Many of us will have reached our own crisis points as mothers; a point where we have been forced to say, 'Enough! I can't do it this way any more. Something has to change!' Perhaps your crisis point has been triggered by a long commute which has been slowly draining you of energy, a difficult family relationship or an illness. Maybe you have been constantly flitting between roles and responsibilities and there isn't enough of you to go around. To surrender our will to God's means to consent to his supremacy in all things. We may not like it but we are willing to will it.[15]

Nikki, mum to Joel, eleven, and Cameron, seven, had to surrender to God in the light of her ill health:

> I had cancer when our youngest was a year old and this was probably my biggest challenge, not just because I didn't know if I was going to live or die and how traumatic that was with small children and a husband, but the devastating feeling that I had let them all down by getting cancer in the first place. I'd always wanted to bring the boys up as radical Christians and I was devastated to think that this might not be possible if I died. They wouldn't ever have really known me or remembered me. It was a really hard but good lesson in teaching me that God is in control, that it's not just about me doing things in my own strength, and to truly trust it all to him.

At these times, we have a choice to make. Will we choose to surrender our own will, discern God's will and follow him? Or will we shrink away in fear, carrying on in the same, unhealthy patterns or thought-processes, and come back to crisis point again?

'Going a little farther, [Jesus] fell with his face to the ground and prayed, "My Father, if it is possible, may this cup be taken from me. Yet not as I will, but as you will"' (Matthew 26:39). In the Garden of Gethsemane we see Jesus experiencing strong, intense emotions, just like us. He understands what it means to be in turmoil. Sweating blood (Luke 22:44), and with his 'soul overwhelmed with sorrow to the point of death' (Matthew 26:38), he is going through agony which none of us will ever fully comprehend.

How does he deal with this intense grief? Firstly, he prays. His body is poised in surrender, face to the ground. He prays: 'May this cup be taken from me.' This cup is his suffering and death on the cross. He does not want to face what the Father has called him to do.

Secondly, he chooses to surrender to his Father in obedience and participate in accomplishing his will in the world. 'Yet not as I will, but as you will.' Jesus was totally focused on his mission to bring liberation to humankind through his death on the cross. So he relinquishes his destiny to his Father. It is surrender at the deepest level.

Jesus prays and surrenders in order that he might complete the mission the Father has for him. His example is one we can follow.

I am poor and needy
Let me take you back to my crisis point. As Micah's screams assaulted my ears, I did not feel like praying. When we reach a crisis point as mums, we often don't feel like praying because praying is the first step towards admitting that we can't handle this alone.

Prayer brings us to humbly admit our neediness. This is a necessary foundation for mission. We need to know that we too are needy, not just those we serve. In crisis, can we reflect that it is not just non-Christians who are in need of the power of the gospel, but us too? We are 'work in progress', being transformed daily into the likeness of Christ. We must allow the gospel to reach every part of us, especially those parts of us which resist God's healing.

Psalm 70:5 says:

> Yet I am poor and needy;
>   come quickly to me, O God.
> You are my help and my deliverer;
>   O Lord, do not delay.

The starting place for me was admitting my own emotional and spiritual poverty. I was no missional Wonder Woman. I didn't have the resources to live self-sufficiently, or to give to others as I was trying to do. Had I been giving through a feeling of moral or spiritual superiority, instead of recognizing that we are all broken, yet crafted in the image of God? Unless I admitted this, I was going to be unable to fully love my husband and children or to live missionally. There was no point running a toddler group and parenting course and trying to support friends when my tank was dry.

For you it may be admitting that you can't be on the board of governors at your child's school as well as run the Alpha course. Or it may be about taking a break from a project while your school-age children need you emotionally in the evenings.

Yes, God's power is made perfect in weakness (2 Corinthians 12:9), but he doesn't expect us to give from a place of bankruptcy. Realizing this was the first step for me towards surrendering and echoing the words of this psalm: 'God, come quickly! I'm desperate!'

Just as I longed for the goodness of the gospel to reach the hearts of my children and those who didn't know Jesus, I needed to recognize that God had a mission to the 'unreached' parts of my heart, to the sources of my ambition, to my fear of people's opinions and to my difficulty in accepting help. I wanted to allow him free rein, not just for my benefit but for my children and those I sought to love in the community as I modelled what it meant to follow Jesus.

I am not alone

This realization of my own neediness didn't come to me as I sat alone in a room with my Bible. When I did that, I just wallowed in self-pity. My husband encouraged me to have a few days of 'retreat' time away to speak and pray with older, wiser mums who had grown-up children – three 'survivors' who had lived through the same battles and had war wounds to show for it. I also spoke to my prayer partner, and to a single friend. So often, we think that the crisis we are going through has never been experienced by anyone else. We fall into a pit of hopelessness and isolation. We fear being honest and appearing desperate, but this fear keeps us from the very thing that can free us – the encouragement, perspective and prayers of others.

Through speaking to my three mum survivor friends, I gained a perspective that I couldn't have come to alone – I realized how common my experiences of exhaustion and doing too much were. I no longer felt alone. I listened to how they had dealt with similar crises. Through my prayer partner and single friend I experienced an overwhelming sense of God's grace. I realized, 'God is really with me in this.'

Do we realize the richness of experience that is around us to draw on? Are there mothers, grandmothers, extended family or friends who we can share with and listen to in our dark times? Can we give God a chance to speak through them?

The beginnings of transformation

When I admitted my own neediness and allowed God to speak to me through others, I began to change. As we begin the process of surrendering we allow God the space to speak to us and transform us. For me, the change came through learning to live in the 'Belovedness' that comes from God, being more honest about my weaknesses and learning how to receive from others.

Living as the Beloved

Stop and reflect for a moment on this profound verse from 1 John 3:1 (NIV1984): 'How great is the love the Father has lavished on us, that we should be called children of God!'

You are God's beloved child. That's a difficult truth to grapple with when you are living out of a sense of duty, trying to earn love and please others. Sometimes our overactivity and inability to say 'no' to people can be motivated by guilt and fear. We fear letting people down, we fear what people will think of us or our children, and we feel guilty about our decisions. Guilt and fear are paralyzing and seem to follow us mums around wherever we go. Knowing we are beloved children of God begins to release us from their grip.

In Gethsemane Jesus could only pray prayers of honesty and surrender because his identity was established as one loved by his Father. It wasn't threatened by Peter who tried dissuading him from going to Jerusalem to fulfil his mission (Mark 8:33) or by the sleepiness of his disciples in the garden.

Joan, mum to Tina, two, shares here a beautiful picture of the Father's love through her reflections on how her husband and daughter interact:

> The most amazing and beautiful thing that I have learned since having children, I have learned from my husband Jim. My own father has always been distant and emotionally detached and so for many years the fatherhood of God meant almost nothing to me. I didn't know what a father's love could look like until I saw my daughter, asleep on her father's lap, blissfully relaxed and safe. I see her laughing with joy as she rides on his shoulders up to college to see me, and saying 'Oh my daddy' with a big delighted grin. I see Jim gently washing her hair, patient, despite her vociferous complaints.

This is what our heavenly Father is like. I asked myself, 'How can I allow this head knowledge to infiltrate my whole being so that everything I do flows out of this truth?' I started by saying the words 'I am God's beloved' several times a day, especially when fear kicked in and I was tempted back to my unnecessary frenzy of housework or when my anxiety left me with little grace to deal with the children. Although I probably sounded a little crazy, it began to have the effect of transforming and renewing my mind (Romans 12:2) by enabling me to see myself as valued by God and therefore deserving of care. Amazingly, just by saying these words aloud, my actions began to change.

I started caring for myself better, resting when I needed to (even if the kids were running riot and I felt guilty), and eating and drinking better (even if I felt there wasn't time). I began to see that God was interested in my physical wellbeing. Over time this extended to the love I was able to show others – I felt moved to handwrite a note of encouragement to a friend, and to lavish love on my daughter during a mummy-daughter date at a coffee shop.

How would knowing you are his beloved transform you? Can you even imagine the freedom of living this way, of doing everything from a sense of being loved – helping your children with their homework, praying for a work colleague, organizing a party for a lonely friend, doing the church finances or picking up some fresh flowers for an elderly relative. This is mission as God intended.

Imagine a life as a disciple of Jesus, lived out of a sense of being valued by God. Imagine if every action you did came from a desire to bless others as you have been blessed. Imagine if every word you said, every decision you made, flowed from the security of being God's beloved child and wanting others to experience the same thing.

Being honest, learning to receive

As I began to live with this awareness, another transformation started to take place. I was able to be more honest with people. I realized that one of the reasons why I had come to my crisis point was because I had allowed a residue of unaired grievances to build up in my relationships due to fear. Could I begin to be regularly honest with others about my thoughts and feelings?

I had a significant conversation with a friend of mine, where I was honest about my opinion instead of pretending that I felt the same way she did. I was extremely nervous about the conversation but found that in reality my fear was unnecessary and I felt better afterwards. I began to practise this discipline of honesty.

Azariah and I also wrote an honest email to a group of our friends who were part of our children's 'Life Village' (for more about this concept, see chapter 9), about how hard we were finding things, and we asked them for help. It was one of the hardest emails I've ever sent. I was petrified before pressing 'Send'. It felt as if I was kicking 'fear' hard in the teeth! I found myself thinking, 'Will they think less of me?' Some of them may have, but the majority offered support in a variety of ways, which was amazing – but which led to our next challenge.

When we find the courage to ask for help and people offer it to us, we then have the opportunity to accept that help, despite possible feelings of guilt. This is easier said than done. Have people offered to make you meals, pick up your children from school or give you something that you really need or want? Receiving help from others isn't selfish. It requires humility and a sense of how valued we are.

The giving and receiving of help is what builds friendships and communities. It is part of mission. We all need each other. There will also be times when we will be the ones offering help to others. If we feel that mission is all about us serving people, giving to others and never receiving anything back, then our relationships will be one-sided. Allowing people to give to us helps them grow too. So we thankfully accepted the help we were offered.

Some additional solutions to our crisis were also needed. Azariah and I prayed together about what these could be. The solution was a combination of extra support for our family, using childcare for a set period of time, me stopping certain activities at church, and an ongoing commitment to working out what it meant for us to be a family on mission. Our situation didn't change overnight but we were taking significant steps in the right direction.

Crafting a family day of rest
Alongside these changes we were making, God was challenging us as a family to rest; to take seriously God's commandment to

have a weekly Sabbath (Exodus 20:9–10). Over time we have crafted our own family Sabbath day, which starts with a special meal, prayer and song in the evening and ends the following tea-time, following the Jewish pattern. We have worked hard to put boundaries into our day of rest so that we can connect with God and each other. For example, we limit how far we travel to prevent the stress of public transport with two young children. Our simple day of rest often involves local parks, lunch in cafés, walks along the canal and playing games. Regular short times of prayer are incorporated and we turn off our phones and don't use the internet.

Sticking to these boundaries is a challenge, especially not using the internet or our phones, but it refreshes us spiritually, prompts thankfulness and strengthens our mission together as a family. We have felt more equipped for the mission God has called us to in our home, church and neighbourhood. Our day of rest means we go out into the week filled with the good things of God rather than working from a deficit. It has created sacred space in our lives – space to enjoy being family, enjoy God's world and enjoy God himself. I have realized how crucial rest is as a foundation for a missional life.

Fruitful mission

Looking back, I can already see some of the fruit that has been borne from the surrender arising from this crisis and the decision to prioritize rest.

Firstly, the two relationships in the community that God had been nudging me towards flourished. My increased energy meant that, when one friend went through a testing time with her own mum and turned up unexpectedly at church, I had enough capacity to support her. We grew closer as a result and the friendship between our children blossomed. My own honesty in telling the other friend how we were struggling inspired her to be more honest about her own struggles and to determine to ask more frequently for what she needed. Dropping certain activities in order to concentrate on others meant that Azariah and I were able to invest more deeply into giving our children attention.

Surrendering to God can lead to mission that flourishes. Perhaps for you it will lead to an awareness of the one thing that God has put in front of you to do now, rather than of six possibilities. Perhaps it will lead to deeper investment into a relationship rather than a task, an old project rather than a new one, or a decision which doesn't seem to make intellectual sense but is perhaps God's way for you now? Perhaps it means acceptance of your personal circumstances rather than anger? In prayerful reflection, can you begin to detect how God is leading you out of your crisis moment to a new place of fruitfulness?

Ruth, mum to Zoe, four, and Phoebe, two, talks about surrendering to God by allowing him to form our characters in the often mundane, relentless, emotional reality of everyday life as a parent:

> I find the relentlessness of it all a constant struggle: the draining housework, where you are running just to stand still, the tiring emotional demands of little ones – one minute happy, the next minute distraught – then going to bed not knowing whether you will get a good night's rest. Surrendering to God means allowing all the ups and downs of family life to really do the deep work of forming me in Christ-likeness.

Surrendering looks different for us all, but it will always lead to becoming more Christ-like. For some it may mean giving up a career; for others it may mean starting a career. For some it may mean deciding to look after ourselves better and for others it may mean looking after others better. Some mums may be led to speak up more and others may be led to shut up more! Choosing God's way is what we are all called to do. Working out what that looks like in everyday life is the challenge for each of us.

The death of Missional Wonder Woman

And so we return to the Wonder Woman mug, which was always my cup of choice for that essential early morning coffee. Alas. It is now lying in a thousand white, blue and red pieces at the bottom of a dustbin. I smashed it. The mug which represented the old, driven, self-sufficient Anna is no more.

My desire to live uncompromisingly and authentically as a godly woman of influence is still very much alive. I still long to use the gifts God has given me to their fullest extent and to be a cheerleader for other women wanting to do the same. But instead, my desires and dreams are beginning to flow from a place of knowing that I'm God's beloved, being honest, learning to receive from others, and prioritizing rest. Why? Because I know that part of God's mission is my own transformation into a Wonder-Ful Woman, equipped to change the world, minus the superhero cape, but still with the thighs.

Questions for exploration

1. Are there things that God is asking you to surrender to him at the moment? If so, spend some time thinking and praying about how guilt or fear may be holding you back.
2. What is the greatest challenge for you at the moment? Living as God's beloved? Being honest with people? Or learning to receive from others? What one step can you take towards one of these this week?
3. Surrendering to God is an ongoing process. How could you and your family commit to this? What effect would it have on mission?

TALES FROM THE FRONTLINE

Ruth

(mum to Anna-May, seventeen, Tom, fifteen, and Maisie, eight)

Ruth and Jon have been married for nineteen years. Ruth originally trained as a primary school teacher, but, after having her eldest two children, decided to be a stay-at-home mum. In 2005 Ruth and Jon adopted Maisie. In 2006 the family took in a teenage mother and her toddler, and in 2008 they became foster carers of babies for the local council. Encouraged by Ruth and her family, other Christians in their wider church family have also become foster carers, creating a burgeoning network of Christian foster carers who can support each other.

We were motivated to become foster carers by a mixture of influences: my dad grew up in care so I've always had an awareness of the care system. I have close friends who are adopted. Also, we adopted our youngest child, and I was so thankful that she had spent her whole time in care with one family who had loved her to bits. That was such a blessing to us. When we moved to a bigger house, we had space – we realized that we could do that for somebody else.

It was like a godly nudge. I knew that a new phase was coming, but at first I didn't know what it was. We had always wanted to go abroad and do mission, but God was showing us that there was something we could do right here and now.

We foster babies because it's an age group I love. I know I've got a lot to give. You can put in place so much with babies. We had the first little boy we fostered for two years, from when he was three months old. He has been adopted now and he insists that his parents pray with him every night! His adoptive mum has said that there are traits and characteristics that she can see in him because she knows that he's had the time and the love that we were able to give him. That's a real blessing and it's one of the things we were keen to do. We wanted to leave children with a Bible, and with a solid foundation for who they are going to become set in place.

It hit me massively when we first started fostering that we were joining a community of people who were doing what Jesus asked us to do, whether they knew it or not. In the Bible we're told to care for widows and orphans, and although these children aren't orphans in the physical sense, they're generally orphans in the emotional sense; they don't have a loving model of parenthood. It struck me what a difference it would make if people in the church were consistently called to serve the city in that way. In our church, much of the talk has been about being a light to the city, and it made me think it would be great if Christians got a reputation in the city for being fabulous foster carers.

It's so easy to look at other mums doing things that you couldn't do and think, 'I must be rubbish then.' The most important thing is to do what God has called you to do. The longing of our heart is to see children with their lives turned round, so that they can take something away that will set them up with a stable understanding of what family life is.

7. MISSIONAL WOMANHOOD: SOURDOUGH AND SISTERHOOD

By Joy

> *Love each other with genuine affection, and take delight in honouring each other.*
> (Romans 12:10 NLT)

For a brief time last year, I had a new man in my life. He was a complicated guy, who made exacting demands, and required frequent attention in order to survive. I looked after him as well as I could, but there were times when I wondered whether he and I would make it. His name was 'Herman the German'.

Some of you may have encountered Herman already. He's a yeast-based sourdough mix, often given out by a kindly friend with a set of instructions. After ten days of mixing, covering and adding sugar, you will marvel at his growth from a pallid mixture at the bottom of a bowl into a bubbling mass of energy that is ready to be mixed with a variety of ingredients and baked into a delicious cake. Herman is a 'friendship cake', a sort of community 'chain-cake' baking exercise. Before you make your own cake at the end of the ten-day cycle, the mixture will have trebled or quadrupled in size. You split the mixture into portions, and give them to friends, neighbours and passers-by in the street who you hope will take Herman off your hands and lavish upon him the attention he has come to expect.

Herman is a powerful image of the way that the kingdom of God is at work in our hearts, lives and communities. In a one-line parable in Matthew's Gospel, Jesus says, 'The kingdom of heaven is like yeast that a woman took and mixed into about thirty kilograms of flour until it worked all through the dough' (Matthew 13:33).

The fantastic thing about this image is the almost unstoppable way that yeast works. Yeast is alive, and, when mixed with the right ingredients, growing is what it does. I love the way that Jesus is putting the language of the kingdom into the primary domain of a first-century woman here. I'm pretty sure baking bread wasn't a big occupation of men in Jesus' time, so we can be sure Jesus wanted women hearing this to know they had a critical role in the growth and spread of his kingdom; an idea that would have been utterly counter-cultural in his day.

Our church plant met on the weekend I was due to make my Herman cake. I knew what we needed to do: inspired by the verse above, we would give our community of new Christians some real-life experience of kingdom growth. Armed with a stack of Tupperware, and briefly explaining Jesus' parable, we handed out our baby Herman to our baby Christians, and told them to expect impressive things.

It was fascinating to see what became of these fledgling mixtures. Some people were full of self-doubt and anxiety at the prospect of raising their batch. Others killed the mix stone dead with neglect. One friend, a brand-new Christian, developed an industrial-scale Herman factory, raising several mixes at a time and distributing them around the community with missionary zeal. We quickly learned who the growing evangelist in our midst was! The whole experience was a fun but profound insight into God's missionary heart. Like yeast, God's mission has a life of its own; his kingdom grows because that's what it's designed to do. Like the sweet and satisfying gift of a cake, his good news is a great gift to us.

There is a simplicity that comes with the recognition that the growth of the kingdom of God is not something that we're supposed to strain over. Herman is pretty hard to kill, because everything in it is surging towards growth and life and energy. These things are what it's destined to do; they're in its DNA.

Herman got me thinking: does the kingdom of God at work in us operate in a similar way? God's Spirit propels us to embrace a life that is ever bubbling up, growing in love, hope, truth, faith and grace.

Kingdom meets normal: The collision of heaven and earth

> People see you at your worst; screaming at the kids or losing them or something else crazy! When they see you at your least composed or in floods of tears because of a mishap, it's humbling. I always try to be as real as possible so that it's not a shock for people when they see me like this and I pray like crazy that somehow God will break through my muddle.
>
> (Jennet, mum to Ben, eight, Archie, six and Millie, four)

It can feel as though our patterns of eating, sleeping, working, child-rearing normality define our lives. Ultimately, though, the kingdom of heaven is on the move, and this redefines them. All around us, bubbling up like yeast in the dough, people are loving truth, seeking justice, hungering for righteousness, questioning, seeking and searching out the One who loves them with an unending love. Heaven and earth are colliding every moment, right in the midst of fraught, workaday ordinariness.

As mothers, this presents us with both momentous pressure and incredible opportunity. How do we become women who walk this world with feet firmly planted on the earth and hearts rooted in the heavens above? In the course of researching this book, I've begun to read mum-bloggers from around the world. As I've done this, I've sensed a collective heartbeat from these diverse and inspirational women. It's been refreshing to find a sisterhood out there, women who are not only passionate about their families and raising their children, but who are also utterly committed to issues of poverty and justice the whole world over. (Check out the appendix for links to fantastic blog sites by some inspirational women.) Could it be that true sisterhood, true motherhood, is much more than caring for our own little family in our own corner of the earth? Can we catch a vision of motherhood and sisterhood that ushers in the bubbling, untamable kingdom in the lives of families we are never likely to meet, whose lives couldn't be more different from our own?

We women are often our own worst enemies. We have so much to learn from each other and yet so often we are stopped by toxic emotions that rob us of passion, energy and good desires: envy, guilt, shame, fear, bitterness – I could go on. These emotions never yield to yeast-like growth and flourishing. As women, we all too often participate in a silent conspiracy that allows these places to fester, unchallenged in the dark corners of our souls.

Let's think about envy for a moment.

For me, it started early. I had been an overweight child, and I remember being painfully aware even in junior school of my body shape and how it differed from most of my friends. It was puppy fat, so I thinned out. In secondary school I worked hard on shaping my image and personality so that comparisons would be kind to me and place me nearer the top of the tree than the bottom. I worked at this with focus and dedication.

I encountered the living God at fourteen, and he gently drew me into a security that was founded on deeper things than the 'hot or not' lists in *Just 17*.

I grew up, got married, had a baby and embarked on this voyage called 'motherhood'.

When I emerged from the zombie-like state that is 'the newborn stage', I began to look all around me at other mothers trying to work out how to do this thing. I felt as though I had joined a club where everybody else but me knew what to do. I loved my son with an intensity I had never before experienced, and I loved observing his emerging personality and getting to know him. The internal world of parenting seemed to be coming together, but as for what it meant to be part of this mums' club, I wasn't so sure.

Harnessing the zeal of my younger days, I began to craft a working model of how best to do this mothering thing. It seemed to be important to tell people when your baby hit a developmental milestone – perhaps this was a marker of the quality of your mothering? In this case, I was in trouble as my baby suffered with allergies and terrible eczema, clung to me like a limpet at toddler groups, and was slow to sit and crawl.

He grew, and so did I. I began to break into my stride. My second baby was an easy baby (it would have been easy to think that this was all about me if I hadn't had my third . . .) and I think it was at about this point that 'Alpha Mother' began to emerge.

Alpha Mother could do things. You need forty cupcakes for the reception class? Not a problem. Want some sleep solutions for your nocturnal infant? In a heartbeat. Alpha Mother rocked up to toddler groups; she attended every school meeting. Alpha Mother had ideas and theories. She was competent. Her home looked nice, she maintained a cool, calm exterior, and enjoyed dining out on stories of her happy, functioning family.

Alpha Mother was a pain. She annoyed people. She once reduced a precious friend to tears of anxiety and incompetence with her superiority. She could be nice enough on the outside, but she couldn't keep people close. Clever, together and consummately strong, she peddled fear and inadequacy and worked hard to keep her many plates spinning.

She sucked the lifeblood out of me. Like Peter Pan's shadow, she lurked in the background, ready to jump out whenever insecurity threatened.

Alpha Mother wanted to grow, and had she done so I suspect she would have slowly suffocated me and then those closest to me. Instead, she is dying. I would like to say she is dead and buried, but I would be lying if I didn't say that she occasionally rears her ugly head.

The problem with Alpha Mother was that she was utterly unaware of her need of a Saviour. She was entirely self-made; a construct defined by her capacity to project success. Alpha Mother and those like her are born when we attempt to botch and patch together for ourselves an identity which will mask our most vulnerable places, instead of turning over our failures to the restorative hands of the King of Love.

What reckless stupidity!

We have in Jesus a Saviour who came not for the healthy, but for the sick. He came to shine his life-giving, radiant light into those dark and secret corners.

As women we are too often willing to collude with one another in the perpetuation of our broken identities. We don't want to see our own sin and pain exposed, so we don't expose anyone else's. I can bring Alpha Mother to the party, Anna could bring Wonder Woman, and together they could share drinks and make small-talk while broken hearts fester and a broken world burns.

Can we begin to catch a vision of how to do this differently? Could we drag our ugly alter-egos into the open daylight of our Father's presence where they will shrivel, and we can shake off their weight and move freely?

Even as I write, I remember the ways that I have maligned the life-giving value of my sisters over the years. Yet when we lay down the insecurities that hold us back, we unearth a treasure trove in our friendships that can spur us on.

All of our relationships can be conduits through which we receive blessing and become a better version of ourselves, or they can drain us and leave us depleted. I'm focusing on our woman-to-woman relationships here, because when there is a culture of women who challenge, champion and cheerlead one another, we see amazing things.

I'm thinking of the women from a church near me, who joined together to develop 'Baby Basics', an amazing initiative providing vital essential equipment for asylum-seeking new mums and their babies which you can read about in Hannah's 'Tales from the frontline' on p. 93.

I'm thinking about Ruth and the group of Sheffield mums who committed to support one another in community as they foster vulnerable babies.

I'm thinking about a group of my friends who decided to bless their children's teachers during an OFSTED inspection by taking prayer requests from each teacher and baking for the teachers during the inspection.

Part of a bigger story?

The problems that we have as women, the ways that we get drawn into comparison and competition, are complicated, but they are not new. There are several precedents for both harmonious and challenging female relationships in the Bible.

In the wonderful Old Testament book of Ruth, we see the way that Ruth remains faithful to her mother-in-law, Naomi, in the most desperate of circumstances. As a Moabite widow, Ruth's choice to return to Israel with Naomi risked a lifetime of hardship, famine and widowhood. While Naomi's other daughter-in-law, Orpah, is persuaded to stay in Moab and take her chances at building a new life, Ruth declares to Naomi,

> Don't urge me to leave you or to turn back from you. Where you go I will go, and where you stay I will stay. Your people will be my people and your God my God. Where you die I will die, and there I will be buried. May the LORD deal with me, be it ever so severely, if even death separates you and me.
> (Ruth 1:16–17)

Ruth is rightly lauded as a biblical heroine, but as her incredible story unfolds, we might easily lose sight of the ordinariness of this asylum-seeking widow. Who could have imagined that Ruth's choice to remain faithful to her destitute mother-in-law would lead her to become the great-grandmother of King David and an ancestor of Jesus?

We see another female relationship when we encounter two very different sisters and their interaction with Jesus when he stays in their home. Martha is busy cooking and preparing her home for their guests, while her sister Mary sits at the feet of Jesus, listening attentively. Over time, Martha's frustration with her sister builds until she finally cracks:

> 'Lord, doesn't it seem unfair to you that my sister just sits here while I do all the work? Tell her to come and help me.'
>
> But the Lord said to her, 'My dear Martha, you are worried and upset over all these details! There is only one thing worth being concerned about. Mary has discovered it, and it will not be taken away from her.'
>
> (Luke 10:40–42 NLT)

The gospel accounts show us that these sisters were as different as chalk and cheese. Martha is a busy, bustling home-owner. In John's Gospel, we find her, practical as ever, sending word to Jesus to come quickly when her brother Lazarus is taken ill, and going out to meet Jesus eagerly when he arrives after Lazarus has died. Importantly, Martha is only the second person in the Gospels (and the first woman) to declare that Jesus is the Son of God (John 11:27).

Mary seems to be quieter and more reflective. The story we read above presents Mary sitting intently at the feet of Jesus, hanging on his every word. This would have been almost unheard of in Jesus' time. The idea of a woman sitting at the feet of a respected rabbi would have been frowned upon. Imagine, then, the scandal when quiet Mary cracks open a jar of perfume worth a year's salary, and pours it on Jesus' feet, wiping it with her hair:

Six days before the Passover celebration began, Jesus arrived in Bethany, the home of Lazarus – the man he had raised from the dead. A dinner was prepared in Jesus' honour. Martha served, and Lazarus was among those who ate with him. Then Mary took a twelve-ounce jar of expensive perfume made from essence of nard, and she anointed Jesus' feet with it, wiping his feet with her hair. The house was filled with the fragrance.

But Judas Iscariot, the disciple who would soon betray him, said, 'That perfume was worth a year's wages. It should have been sold and the money given to the poor.' Not that he cared for the poor – he was a thief, and since he was in charge of the disciples' money, he often stole some for himself.

Jesus replied, 'Leave her alone. She did this in preparation for my burial. You will always have the poor among you, but you will not always have me.'

(John 12:1–8 NLT)

These sisters loved and supported Jesus during his ministry. They opened up their home and hearts to him; they had watched their brother die and seen him raised from the dead. Now they are facing the loss of their dear friend Jesus to a horrific death as well.

When we first encounter Martha and Mary, we feel the full force of Martha's frustration with her sister, but in this account, the sisters appear to be more secure in their different identities. Martha is still serving others, but without angst and agitation. Mary is making a bold statement at the feet of Jesus, but this time her sister doesn't seem to judge her. Could it be that these sisters have learned that they are equally precious in Jesus' eyes, even though their characters are so different?

Theologian Elisabeth Moltmann-Wendell says, 'If Mary is the embodiment of reflective, contemplative Christianity, Martha is the embodiment of active Christianity . . . Of course women will always be different. The only problem will be if all of them follow the same model.'[16]

Ladies, God takes delight in our diversity. The world would be so impoverished if there was just one standard type of Christian woman, and yet we so often live as though this is the case. What a two-dimensional, narrow way to think!

I have friends who wear their babies all day long, and friends who time their baby's routines with a clock. Some like to make outrageous statements just to stir things up, and some wouldn't say boo to a goose. Some are creative and impulsive; some delight in order and routine. I often see things that I like about my friends, things that I, sadly, lack; but I am learning that these observations present me with a choice: envy and insecurity, or cheerleading and celebration.

I am slowly and surely embracing the discipline of making the second choice.

I am learning that I cannot, should not and will not ever be 'everywoman'. It is so easy to believe that we should each have a glittering career, sweet-natured children, a beautiful home, a romance-filled marriage, a wide array of interesting friends, a multiplicity of creative talents, time to spare, holidays abroad, a fabulous wardrobe, a gorgeous figure, no grey hair . . . I could go on . . . for a long time. Add into this our 'Alpha-Christian' expectations: that we might have an inspiring devotional life, capacity to care for the needy, leadership skills, powerful gifts of evangelism and wisdom, fruitfulness across all areas of our lives and that all of this would be beautifully recorded in our fascinating blog.

My head is reeling from all of this pressure.

We need to take a collective deep breath and remind ourselves that we are not supposed to have it all, do it all or be it all. We are a small part of a glorious whole, made to be in community, complemented and strengthened by the diversity of others.

When we moved into our house ten years ago, I had all kinds of plans for how I would organize my kitchen. The moving day was crazy, and by the time I eventually made it into the kitchen my lovely girlfriends had unpacked everything and decided where it all would go. Momentarily, my inner control-freak surfaced, and I felt threatened by their über-competent domesticity. I needed to stop and have a word with myself: their help was actually a tremendous blessing. They were much more practical and had better systems than mine. My kitchen was now organized! It was time to admit that the combined strength of the sisterhood had won out over my insecurity-driven need to be in control. I love the freedom that comes with the realization that while I am rubbish at organizing kitchen cupboards (there are things that have lain dormant in their recesses these ten long years), there are others who have these skills. Together, we can be awesome!

I am determined to walk a path that is intent on building up, delighting in and cheerleading my sisters, because I cannot be effective in the mission field God has for me alone. Going back to Herman swelling proudly in his bowl, we are reminded that the kingdom of God is also bubbling away all around us. God is busy at work, whether we know and see it or not, at the school gates, in our office, on our street, in our friends, our family – he is on the move. Do we have hungry hearts, eyes to see and ears to hear all that God is doing?

When we are gripped by toxic emotions, when our energy is spent on comparing ourselves with other women, and on envy, it becomes really hard to live in a missional way.

These undisclosed states of the heart can be a dirty little secret that we keep to ourselves. The problem with this is that while we are languishing in the familiarity of our insecurity, we are missing opportunities to bless, serve, love and reach out. If left unchallenged, these dark corners grow, crowding out our desires to see God's kingdom spread and flourish. What can we do to reverse this?

Name and shame
'Therefore confess your sins to each other and pray for each other so that you may be healed. The prayer of a righteous person is powerful and effective' (James 5:16).

Our unresolved feelings, if left hidden, will run rampant. It is freeing to call them what they are. The sickening emotions that seem so overwhelming in our minds are made smaller when we speak them out. When unconfessed to our heavenly Father and others, our emotions control us. Naming and shaming the powerful emotions that hold us back can set us free.

Whose wardrobe do you envy? Whose figure do you wish for? Who are you most threatened by? Whose parenting do you judge? What do you undervalue about yourself? What do you overvalue?

Call these things out, write them down, repent of them, laugh about them with a friend and rob them of their power over you! He has made us for so much more than this.

Be thankful

'So then, just as you received Christ Jesus as Lord, continue to live your lives in him, rooted and built up in him, strengthened in the faith as you were taught, and overflowing with thankfulness' (Colossians 2:6–7).

Thankfulness has a power all its own. It is easy to think it is just a nice thing to try, a way to airbrush all that is hard in life, but it isn't. Thanksgiving is a discipline. It is an exercise in perspective-shifting, moving from a focus on the negative to the positive. It is the choice to embrace realities that might otherwise remain unseen while we are blinded by worries, cares and complexities.

What could you be thankful for today? Start with right where you are: the place that you sit, the food that you have eaten, the conversations you have had, the clothes you wear, the roles you have in life, the people who mean something to you, the beauty you see in nature . . . your list could be endless. I am inspired by the writer Ann Voskamp, who decided to write a list of one thousand things she was grateful for. The process saw her perspective on life, her relationship with God and with others transformed.[17]

Embarking on a journey of thankfulness means choosing to celebrate the gifts that are right in front of you, even now. It is not easy to make that choice when the journey is slow, but as we choose to be thankful, our perspective shifts and our negative attitudes loosen their grip on us.

Become a cheerleader

'Let us consider how we may spur one another on toward love and good deeds' (Hebrews 10:24).

Have you ever had a friendship with another woman that was cultivated in the hot-house of mutual insecurity? These relationships are fraught and difficult to navigate. The benefits of the relationship can be lost at any moment due to an ill-timed comment or a wrongly received gesture.

While we all have our insecurities, and even our closest friends may push our buttons at times, there is a different way for female friendship that brings freedom and joy. It requires the conscious choice to challenge the negativity of our own insecurities, and to embrace the call to be cheerleaders of the women around us.

Becoming a cheerleader for other women is truly liberating. It enables us to see gifts and talents in others that are different from our own. It reminds us that we are a small part of a bigger whole. It shows us that we can achieve more when we realize that we are a team.

Cheerleading others is a crucial part of a life on mission. It is like the oxygen in the soil that makes the ground fertile. In an atmosphere fuelled by competition how can mission possibly flourish? When we are able to take genuine pleasure in our diverse friendships, the choice to celebrate and cheerlead our friends will change us from the inside out.

I love the way that we are all so different: each one of us reflecting different aspects of the Father's identity, but none of us perfect. We have different stories to tell, different gifts and talents, different perspectives and values. We can all learn so much from one another.

I have been inspired when I have seen women working together on the missional frontline, supporting one another and using their God-given skills to further his kingdom. Over the years, I have often heard Christian author and leader, Mary Pytches, talk of her friendship and ministry partnership with her friend Prue Bedwell. I asked Mary about how they have cultivated this friendship and working relationship:

Prue and I worked together for a little over twenty years out of the same church. We were close friends as well as co-workers. I knew from my years on the mission field that relationships between women can be fraught with problems, stemming from insecurity, so from the beginning we were aware of the possible pitfalls. We decided from the first that openness and honesty was the way forward. We soon realized that, though our work was similar, our gifting was different and that, providing we gave each other the space and freedom to do the things we were good at, we were actually complementary and the end result was so much better than if either of us tried to go it alone.

Though it might have appeared at first that I was the main speaker and that Prue was playing second fiddle to me, in fact that was never the case. She was vital to all that we did and I could never have managed the travelling and stress of speaking and ministering if she had not been by my side. Over the years she became a very competent speaker herself and gradually took her fair share of the platform. It was by God's grace that feelings of competition and jealousy were never a problem.

I personally owe a huge amount to Prue. We ministered together in many different countries and had some memorable experiences, some of which would have been hard to handle on one's own but together were made bearable, even hilarious. I count our friendship as one of God's great blessings and it was an added bonus that our friendship appears to have been a blessing to others.

The passage in Ecclesiastes 4:9 describes our relationship well.

Two are better than one,
    because they have a good return for their labour.
If either of them falls down,
    one can help the other up.
But pity anyone who falls
    and has no one to help them up . . .
Though one may be overpowered,
    two can defend themselves.
A cord of three strands is not quickly broken.

This shows how God can powerfully use female friendship as a missional resource when we resolve to surmount insecurity and envy, and champion one another.

Our heavenly Father is alongside us on our journey, whispering encouragement, always championing his girls. We have an advocate in heaven (Job 16; John 14; 15; 16; 1 John 2) who cheers us on.

Our mission will go from strength to strength when we realize the freedom unleashed as we cheerlead one another. Have our dreams been too small, our bar set too low, because our vision has been limited by our solitary perspective?

It is time for us to embrace a Herman-like understanding of growth and possibility as the kingdom of God is unleashed through the lives of women just like us. As our weakness is supported by his strength, we will be transformed into an unassailable force. Let's laugh together, wives, mothers and daughters, at the days to come (Proverbs 31).

Questions for exploration

1. Can you name one toxic emotion that has had an impact on you? How has it damaged your relationship with God? How has it impacted your relationship with other women?

2. How could you begin to embrace the discipline of thankfulness?
3. What would it mean for you to commit to cheerleading your sisters? What practical steps might you take to live this out?

Jane

(mum to Dan, eighteen, Lucy, sixteen, and Anna, twelve)

Jane runs her own image consultancy business, True Colours, and has her own brand of cosmetics (see www.janefardon.com).

I've been an image consultant for about twenty years. I was drawn to it because it was a way of bringing together a variety of things that were really important to me: my faith, wanting to affirm women, teaching and communication, and art and creativity. It felt like a really easy way to express my faith as well as add to the family income.

When our children were small, we moved around a lot for my husband's job, so I didn't do image consultancy as a profession; it was more of a ministry. I gave demonstrations on choosing your best colours with mums and toddlers groups, or shared my story and some of my skills at a church event.

As a teenager, I didn't feel confident. I loved dressing up, but that didn't translate into confidence in the outside world. I am quite small, and I don't have a 'standard' figure, so all the things that my teenage friends wore looked so much better on them than they did on me! As a result I never felt very comfortable in my skin; I always felt a bit awkward. Gradually my confidence grew when I became an adult, but training in image really helped me to understand what you do when you don't have a standard figure. My own journey in self-confidence has given me a desire to help women accept themselves and celebrate their God-given beauty.

When we moved to Sheffield and all my children were at school, we set up True Colours. The vision for the business is based on Isaiah 61:3, where we're told that God will 'bestow on [his people] a crown of beauty instead of ashes'. We run individual consultations and group workshops on Colour, Style, Make-up and also Identity. A lot of the women who come are mums who have been bought a session as a gift. They are at home with young children and have lost a sense of who they are.

Before our first child was born, I remember my mum saying to me, 'There's a point in birth where you think you're going to die.' During labour it can feel like death as you birth a new life. Then, when you're a mother, it can feel like part of you has died, and yet so often we make a home in that place of death. We think, 'I don't exist any more, I'm just So-and-so's mum, my figure's gone, my mind's gone, my life's gone.' Our life, and indeed our figures, may have changed, but it's really important that we are still ourselves and realize *we* still matter. If we are going to continue to be life-givers, we have to be alive ourselves and not stay in that dead place. Our children need to be nurtured physically, emotionally and spiritually, but you can only give life out of life. The more we are able to see ourselves as God sees us – to be truly alive – the more we will be able to nurture good self-worth (and many other things) in our children.

I feel called to redeem the beauty industry wherever I can; so much of it is designed to feed our insecurity, which is why people spend so much money on their image and why there's this constant search that is never fulfilled. We need to celebrate the way God has created each woman, saying, 'As you are now, you are beautiful, you are loved and you have a purpose.'

This is what I believe God has called me to do.

8. MISSION AND SUFFERING: WHAT HAPPENS TO MISSION IN A CRISIS?

By Joy

It was 9.30pm on a lovely summer holiday Sunday night when I got the phone call. My best friend Milly was sobbing uncontrollably down the phone, and panic immediately began to rise within my chest. Through her tears she explained that her close friend's four-year-old daughter, Bethany, had just fallen unconscious with some kind of brain injury. Nobody was sure yet what had happened, but the family were being airlifted from Cornwall, where they had been staying with family, to Bristol. Milly and I talked and prayed as she shared the story. It was a life-and-death situation.

Emergency surgery saved Bethany's life, but left her unconscious and on a ventilator. The church community rallied around Alan and Sarah, Bethany's parents. Their elder girls were cared for by friends and family, and groups of people travelled to Bristol to support Alan and Sarah and to pray round the clock for Bethany's recovery. Back in Sheffield, hundreds of people became involved in praying 24/7 for the little girl and supporting her family.

It emerged that Bethany had suffered a bleed in her brain; this has left the cognitive area of her brain completely unscathed, but has damaged the part that controls her motor function. After a year of extensive rehabilitation and recovery, Bethany remains in a wheelchair and on a ventilator. She has very limited motor control, and so is unable to communicate, swallow or move for herself. Despite this, her amazing family ensure that she is surrounded with unceasing love, care and stimulation. In September, she began attending infant school, and last Christmas, she played the part of the star in the school nativity play.

We continue to pray for Bethany's full recovery, and to live with the tension that exists between her disability and our unrelenting hope for healing.

I belong to a different church from Milly, and am on the periphery of the extended community that have supported Alan and Sarah and their family. Despite the deep pain and sadness of this situation, it has been deeply moving to see the transforming power of a worshipping community who have brought together everything at their disposal in order to see the kingdom of God extend its reach even in the darkest of times. Alongside long-term offerings of prayer, food and childcare, Alan and Sarah have had their bedroom redesigned and made over by friends, the children of the church have been mobilized in prayer for their young friend, powerful worship songs have been written, friends have cried, prayed and laughed together, and a church has been changed. People who are not Christians have been involved in most of the above. No-one who has encountered this lovely family and walked even part of this painful journey with them could be left untouched.

But none of this makes what happened OK. None of this should lessen our resolve to go on fighting to see God's kingdom come even more powerfully than we have already seen.

The kingdom of God, his rule and reign over heaven and earth, is a 'now' and a 'not yet' kingdom. As followers of Jesus, we know that his Spirit is at work in our lives; we know that the

Father's love extends to and is available for all, but we don't yet see the kingdom of God in all of its fullness. We long for the day when, as we are told in Revelation, 'He will wipe every tear from their eyes. There will be no more death or mourning or crying or pain, for the old order of things has passed away' (Revelation 21:4).

We live in the knowledge that this is the promise for our future reality. And we live in the tension of waiting and hoping. 'Faith is being sure of what we hope for and certain of what we do not see' (Hebrews 11:1 NIV1984).

We all have those times when horrors seem to crowd in from every angle. Recently our church community has been rocked by two untimely deaths and several bouts of illness. Suffering rightly leads to questions and, like Jacob, we must wrestle these through and may be left with a limp in our gait as a result (Genesis 32).

What happens to mission when we suffer?

The question that I really want to explore as we think about the many painful experiences that either we or our friends are facing is: what happens to mission in the midst of suffering? Is it still possible to live a missional life when things go wrong?

Often, I think we can fall into the unconscious trap of believing that mission is something that we 'do', rather than being a product of who we 'are': the 'sent ones' of Jesus.

If mission is something that we do, then it will inevitably take a back seat when life throws a curve ball. It is easy to fall into the trap of believing that mission is an 'add-on extra' that we do when everything else in our lives is OK. If we think this way, then mission will be the icing on our perfect Christian cake, something that we participate in when our work is settled, our marriage is happy, our children are behaving and the weather is nice.

But what if that day never comes?

What if our lives, characterized by living in the 'now and the not yet' of the kingdom of God, see more of the 'not yet' than the 'now'? Does our suffering, our imperfection and our pain preclude us from being God's 'sent ones', agents of the good news of the kingdom?

While writing this book, and explaining to people what I'm writing about, I've come to see that 'mission' is a topic that can make even mature Christians shift uncomfortably in their seats. We have so many misconceptions about mission, and the way that we engage in it is inevitably changed by these. People are sometimes wary of mission because they don't like to talk about their faith. Often these same people are incredibly loving and sacrificial, naturally drawing others into community, giving them time and commitment, and gently modelling life as a follower of Jesus. They don't think that they're engaged in mission, because they aren't focused on verbalizing the central tenets of Christian theology. This is simply not true. Yes, it's true that we need to proclaim the good news of Jesus with words, but we also need to proclaim it with the rest of our lives.

When we believe that mission is just another activity, part of the Christian to-do list, along with flower arranging and organizing the Christmas fair, then we spectacularly miss the point. Any mission that we do become involved in will potentially have an element of 'us and them'. We might break ranks from the comfort of our cosy church in order to throw a 'gospel grenade' out into the big bad world, but then we retreat back into our safe Christian community, relieved that our duty has been done.

This is such an undignified way for the beautiful bride of Christ to behave. The church was never meant to be our cosy club. Those who have the light of Christ burning within them ought to spearhead transformation and change in every dark corner of our broken world. The church needs to be a compassionate voice that speaks into world events, science, medicine, media, the arts, politics, ecology, care for the vulnerable, and human identity. There should be no world arena left untouched; no place too difficult, no issue too complex for those impacted by the love of Christ to be absent from the conversation.

The church needs to be the place we are sent from, not the place that we retreat to, a hospital for the sick, not a refuge for the saved.

Mission simply cannot be something that we 'do'. Instead, it is an integral part of our identity in Christ, like breathing is an integral part of being human. I'm not entirely sure how Jesus could relate to our sanitized twenty-first-century Christianity, where mission is seen as an extra that we fit in *after* we have secured our safe, comfortable, happy lives.

If mission is who we are, not what we do, then it doesn't stop when life goes wrong. Its form may alter, and its emphasis may shift, but if mission comes out of who we are and what God has done and is doing in our lives, then it continues in even the most pressing circumstances.

I have marvelled as I have watched Alan and Sarah, their family and their community, live this out. The sadness of Bethany's unresolved situation has not left them bitter. They walk a path of real grief, real community and solid hope among the rubble of pain, broken dreams and physical disability. We expect the presence of the kingdom of God to be shiny and perfect and clean, but honestly, I've rarely seen it more than I see it here.

Sarah says,

> I think that if you love Jesus and you're following him, you can't help but be missional. It's like the analogy of salt; you're either good salt or you're bad salt. Whatever is happening in life, and whether you think you're able or not, you're always a witness. I do know people whose circumstances have robbed them of what they had, but I just want the Jesus who is on the inside to be seen on the outside. It's a bit like a stick of rock. My hope is that, wherever you cut me or my family, you will see Jesus. It's about my life, lived out. I know I'm not perfect, and there's more of Jesus that needs to be seen, but you can only give out what's already inside. If you don't know the Father's love, you can't share the Father's love. I really want to know and share the kindness of God.

Now, we don't care what people think of us any more. We know that our God is good, our God is real. In hospital, lives are transparent, so if you're having a row, everyone is listening. Our experience with Bethany was too big to box, so we needed to be open. If we wanted to pray, we would; if we wanted to discuss, we did. One day, a nurse was asking me about the book that I was reading. It was *God on Mute* by Pete Grieg, which addresses the issue of unanswered prayer. The nurse asked, 'Has your perception of God changed through this experience?' I was able to tell her that I didn't have all the answers, that we haven't seen full answers to prayer, but that we have always had an overwhelming sense of God's goodness.

We are constantly holding the tension of knowing that God could heal Bethany at any moment, along with our grief and the reality of what we're facing. We've done practical things. We spent six months with Bethany at the best children's brain injury rehabilitation centre in the UK, and we continue to grieve. Recently, we've been challenged by the idea that not only have we and Bethany been robbed of the life she could have been living, but also God the Father has been robbed, because he has a plan and a purpose for Bethany's life. This has helped us to continue to press in and pray for her full restoration.

Not long ago at bedtime, Ellie, aged eight, said, 'So Mummy, when are all the prayers for Bethany going to work?' The kids have seen us both crying; we've cried together. I just had to say to her, 'I can't answer your question. I don't know when Bethany will be healed, but I do know that God is good. All we know is to trust Jesus. We don't know what else to do.' We wanted our pain to be transparent for the girls. We have pain over this, and it's OK for them to have pain too. They are part of the journey.

Before Bethany got ill, we were leading a missional community, 'Roots', in our children's school. When Bethany got ill, people stepped up all around us, and began to lead the community. People who aren't Christians, whom we and Bethany had never met, came to Roots to pray with the community for our family. In the course of Bethany's illness, we never once thought that God's mission had gone wrong, but I did say to Alan once, 'This seems to be drawing people to God, but I'm not sure that I would recommend it as an evangelism strategy.'

We've been encouraged as we've seen the community coming together. What we were trying to live and model and be to other people before Bethany was ill has come back to us. People have stepped up, been willing.

At times I get frustrated that we're not seeing people move all the way through to full discipleship. My fear is that we could be stuck at the point of people thinking that faith is all about being a nice person. But I recognize that we have an immediate view of mission; instead we have to ask ourselves: what will these families, these relationships and these children look like in twenty years' time?

These powerful words from Sarah demonstrate the way that the kingdom of God is breaking in, even in the midst of real and undeniable pain and suffering. We must, in the midst of our own lives, hold on to the reality that the kingdom and suffering can and do coexist.

Often we feel an intuitive need to separate kingdom and suffering. It is as though we buy into the myth that the kingdom's currency is power and success, while suffering and brokenness run counter to all that we celebrate and value. When we do this, we forget that we serve a suffering King.

The ultimate triumph of the kingdom – our forgiveness, salvation, freedom and the promise of eternity with the Father – was bought by the sacrifice of Jesus' broken body, voluntarily surrendered to unimaginable pain and torture. It was not pretty when his suffering was transformed and the kingdom broke loose, ripping through the curtain of the temple and history itself. Jesus chose the cross and the grave. (I wanted to say he 'embraced' the cross and the grave, but if I read my Bible right, I'm not sure he was that happy about it.)

We're not supposed to glibly minimize, sermonize or shake it off when life falls down around our ears. It's OK to fall down, break down, grieve, stop and reflect. We don't need a defined, systematic theology of why bad stuff happens. We need to meet the suffering King, and allow his kingdom, his presence, his rule and his reign to unfold in the tatters of our lives.

Sharing the gospel when everything is hard

There will be people reading these pages living through illness, divorce, unemployment, debt, bereavement and depression. In these circumstances, sharing the good news of Jesus with others feels like yet another unachievable ideal. How do we square up our call to be disciples and missionaries when our lives don't seem so full of good news?

I recently visited the home of my old friends, Louise and Dave, for the first time. Louise ushered me into their warm and welcoming living room filled with family photos and children's artwork. I had come to hear about the tragic loss of their six-year-old son, Ben. Ben died in April 2011, after a year-long battle with a brain tumour. As Louise charted their journey into places that none of us ever want to go, I was aware that this is a land with no roadmap. We can't know how we would navigate such loss and anguish. Dave had been co-leading a church before Ben became ill; their lives had been full with family life, work and Christian leadership. I wanted to know how they had travelled this dark road with their remaining son, Joe, who's ten. Louise explained:

> During the time that Ben was first poorly, we completely believed that God was going to heal him. We trusted God to heal Ben, and people around us proclaimed, 'We're not going to let Ben die.' When Ben had high-dose chemotherapy, he must have had a virus, and he developed chronic pneumonia. He ended up in intensive care, and after a couple of days we were told that Ben would die. The ventilators weren't working so they had been

resuscitating him manually for half an hour. Dave and our friend Kev had been sending up some desperate prayers in the toilets. Within fifteen minutes Ben was out of immediate danger and back on the ventilator. ICU had never seen anything like it and they talked about it being a miracle. We held on tight to that miracle, believing God would complete what he had started. We had 24/7 prayer support from good friends and from faithful people whom we had never met before. Also, Ben attended a Catholic school who were like an extended family; they were, and still are, such a fantastic support. The parish church next door to school had a 'sanctuary lamp' which stayed constantly lit in Ben's name as people prayed for him. Parents at school said that, if it hadn't been for Ben, they wouldn't have gone back to church. People saw the reality of our faith, and Ben's, and that encouraged them.

Up until the point where Ben got his terminal diagnosis, we felt there was a purpose; other people's lives were being touched. We were reaching new families in the same situation in hospital. We pressed on. After the terminal diagnosis, we began to flounder. It was so hard to make sense of the miracle that Ben got out of ICU and yet the cancer remained. I remember shouting at God in the car. Why was this happening? But in spite of everything, I knew that I didn't want to lose my relationship with God and I didn't want to lose it for Joe as well.

Before Ben got the terminal diagnosis, we had taken every opportunity to have people pray for him. When we eventually went to Bluebell Wood Hospice we felt that it was time to rest, to let go, to enjoy the time we had left. At that point peace descended. We knew that it was in God's hands. We'd chased the miracle because we really wanted to see it happen and believed that it would. Our journey has led us to see that God heals sometimes, not every time. We don't know why.

After Ben's death, friendships that had been just functional fell away. We discovered that the deepest relationships were those where we just shared our lives, kept nothing hidden. Some of my closest friends are friends that were toddler group mums. Most of them don't go to church, but they are the people we've done the deepest journeying with. On reflection, to begin with, it was a safe place where we could share all our pain and doubts without being challenged. But as we have got stronger, these friends are our new extended family, facing each other's challenges together: doing life together. And even more precious is when friends lend us their children to help fill the huge gap in Joe's life now that Ben has died.

I've tried to hold on to the reality of God, and the value of following Jesus because I can't deny that it's true, but now I've got to work with that truth. We didn't talk to God for ages, treading water for a while, but what was true before is still true now. We're now working that out from our new reality and changed theology. Dealing with this is a lot about choice and a desire to keep moving forward. My perspective on life has changed, and death doesn't seem so bad either. Ben being healed versus Ben meeting Jesus we decided was a win-win situation.

We have learned to take risks, to live like we don't know what's round the corner. We take opportunities to be with people, to share what's on our hearts. We have become bolder. More often than not, people want to share in your grief. Most people are hurting, but people don't want to say so. It's amazing what being vulnerable can do in relationships.

Our missionary activity must be born out of the reality of our lives, and how our relationship with Jesus impacts us in fair weather and foul. If mission is dependent upon programmes rather than relationship, we will burn ourselves out when times are hard.

Could it be that Jesus is as much at work through our pain, our loss and our vulnerability as he is in our joy, our plenty and our strength? As Louise found, people all around us are putting on a brave face, working hard every day to keep the machine rolling while turmoil rages inside. We think that the gospel needs to be told in rainbow colours of success and victory, but the dark, brooding watercolours of the cross paint a more powerful picture.

In Colossians 1, Paul describes 'the glorious riches of this mystery . . . kept hidden for ages and generations'. The mystery is simply this: 'Christ in you, the hope of glory' (Colossians 1:26–27).

This mystery is the embodiment in us, followers of Jesus, of the 'now and not yet' kingdom rule of God. Christ is in us. We hope for his glory to be seen fully one day, but we don't see it fully yet. Nevertheless, he is in us and we have reason to hope.

Our hope is not in our own strength and competence, but in Christ alone. It is easy to forget this, because many of us have invested heavily in strength and the skill of 'keeping it together'. If we live this way, during hard times we may find that the pressure to keep up appearances is unbearable. Missional activity becomes another unmanageable demand. It leads us to retreat into the safer confines of family life. The 'baby' of mission gets thrown out with the dirty bathwater.

This isolates us, and limits resources that God uses to draw us back into his presence and advance his kingdom. Sometimes these resources will include our friends who are not yet Christians, as Louise and Dave, and Sarah and Alan discovered.

Are you struggling right now? It could be that you are facing money worries or illness, relationship difficulties or unemployment, depression or doubt. Whatever the situation, are you walking this journey alone, head down and despondent, or are you scanning the horizon for signs that God is still on the move? Will you allow God to meet you in the mess of life, and can you trust that he will hold on to you even when you feel barely able to hold on to him? My friend Carol shares her experience:

> Having a child who has been gravely ill for four years has been the greatest challenge I've faced in life. I have been so angry with God

for allowing this to happen, but have been sustained through the friends, family and church community he has provided. Also I can see that God is using this painful experience to bring freedom to the whole family. There is a bigger picture. When my child became ill I told God that, if he died, it was over for God and me, but I felt that he said, 'Really?' I knew that nothing could separate us!

(Carol, mum to Matthew, seventeen, Joel, fifteen, James, seven, and Ella, three)

This world does not need self-made, self-satisfied, sanitary Christianity. Jesus calls his followers to get messy, to get right into the thick of the blood, sweat and tears of this world. To live lives that are real and transparent, because our transparency makes him visible to everyone else. He is never compromised by our pain or vulnerability: only by our efforts to mask it. When we invite those around us into our reality, we also invite them to share in Jesus' transformative power at work in us.

We may not all be facing life-and-death situations, but we all experience the reality of living in the 'now and not yet' kingdom as suffering and pain assault us and those we love. We don't have to be super-strong and power through whatever comes our way, but can we 'stand' as we're encouraged to do in Ephesians 6:13?

'Therefore put on the full armour of God, so that when the day of evil comes, you may be able to stand your ground, and after you have done everything, to stand.'

Here Paul exhorts disciples of Jesus to equip themselves with truth, righteousness, the gospel of peace, faith, salvation and the Holy Spirit (Ephesians 6:14–17). These might sound like unlikely weapons, but then aren't we unlikely warriors?

The words of Paul in 2 Corinthians 4 say it best:

We have this treasure in jars of clay to show that this all-surpassing power is from God and not from us. We are hard pressed on every side, but not crushed; perplexed, but not in despair; persecuted, but not abandoned; struck down, but not destroyed. We always carry around in our body the death of Jesus, so that the life of Jesus may also be revealed in our body.

(2 Corinthians 4:7–10)

Battle-weary, bruised and broken, some of us may need to be raised to our feet again by our fellow warriors. Standing may use every last reserve we have. The reality is that death and life have always been cohabiting, fighting it out in our souls in this 'now and not yet' existence. Can we hold on to the glorious hope he extends that, one day, he will make everything new (Revelation 21:5) and can we share this hope with others?

Questions for exploration

1. How has suffering and hardship deepened your understanding of and capacity for mission?
2. Could you take some time to pray or journal and ask God to show you the places where his strength can be at work in your weakness?
3. Is there someone you know who is suffering now? How can you extend the love of Jesus to them?

TALES FROM THE FRONTLINE

Faye

(mum to Zach, sixteen, and Gabi, twelve)

Faye lives in Sheffield with her son Zach, aged sixteen. She runs her own marketing and PR training and consultancy business specializing in supporting entrepreneurs and the third sector – voluntary, community and faith groups. Faye's marriage broke down in 2002. She and her husband remained single and parented separately for the next nine years, and in 2011 he took his own life. Faye talks about the challenges of living a missional life as a single parent and running her own business in the midst of both her own and her family's grief.

For me, life is about giving, loving, serving, caring and praying – but I only have so much time and energy to go round. I want to be there for people, so I just do what I can. I have to ask myself, 'What do I have the resources to do today?'

Despite everything, God is still good, and I press on, one foot after another. My business is called 'Keep your Fork', because I believe the best is yet to come. It's like if someone tells you to keep your fork after a meal, it's because something better is coming next – though whether that will be in this life or the next, we don't know. Platitudes, and saying, 'Jesus will make it better', don't help – it may get better or it may not. We don't know. Our challenge is to stay faithful. I think the biggest question for all of us is, 'Did we learn how to love?'

I'm gifted as a pioneering evangelist, so I'm passionate about mission. For me, sharing the gospel is saying, 'I've got something great; would you like it too?'

Christianity is not primarily about learning Scripture, going to church or giving 10% of your income; it's about whether we can love others in the midst of whatever life throws at us, and I can do that. I still have to fight against the residual pain, bitterness and anger and fear; but every day, I can choose to love the Lord and love others, and if I can keep doing that, those things will subside because the love will fill the hole and squeeze the rest out.

All we have is hope. If our current circumstances are all there is, how awful! On any day, our lives can change beyond all recognition. I'm not looking for a new husband, but I could meet one tomorrow. I'm not looking for a new career, but one may come. I'm sure that the more we embrace a life of faith, hope and love, the more God can bless us. While you have closed fists hanging on to the past, you don't have open hands to receive.

I often find that my business clients sit down and tell me their stories of brokenness and desperation, and they ask how I can help them succeed in business. We choose to move on together. It seems I am discipling my clients as we journey together spiritually too. They are rarely Christians. I've had clients who have experienced every sort of abuse, depression, panic attacks, homelessness, addictions, broken adoption, eating disorders – I am privileged to hear their stories, and then we decide together what elements we will share with the world. My clients know that I'm a Christian, and they know that I'm in their corner. I count it a tremendous privilege to tell other people's stories for a living.

I'm not responsible for the results of these conversations, but I am responsible if I only say, 'That's sad – see you.' I have to do my bit and then I'm clean. Our time and our attention is the most valuable thing we can ever give another human being, because we'll never get our time back.

After giving this interview in January 2013, Faye's daughter, Gabi, died suddenly of a suspected seizure in March, aged twelve. Despite her enormous grief, Faye would still like her account to be included here, as her original words hold true in all circumstances. Our thoughts and prayers are with Faye and Zach as they walk this journey.

9. COMMUNITY: FINDING YOUR LIFE VILLAGE

By Anna

> *You can develop a healthy, robust community that lives right with*
> *God and enjoy its results only if you do the hard work of getting*
> *along with each other, treating each other with dignity and honor.*
> (James 3:18 MSG)

The thought made me break into a cold sweat. Butterflies battled for supremacy in my stomach as I contemplated going through this traumatic ordeal and doing it alone. Despite my husband's pleadings, I knew that all alone, I had to . . . make a cake. My daughter's second birthday cake. It was the stuff of nightmares.

Imagine me, a self-defined non-baker, having to find all the right equipment, ingredients and decorating paraphernalia in order to impress ten adults, bring a smile to my little girl's face and convince Azariah that his idea of buying one at the supermarket was beyond foolish. Where on earth should I start? How big should it be? What shape, flavour and icing should I choose? I decided to turn to my mentor, Uncle Google, for a picture I could copy. It was the wrong strategy. It seemed that every cake on the internet had been baked by a mum with champion cake-baking credentials, women who made cupcakes for their nursery teachers when they were three and a half. My quivering knees collapsed into a prayer position and I began to intercede for my troubled soul.

Jesus calmed my stormy heart, and I realized my first objective was to produce a home-made cake. My second objective was to reduce my rising stress levels, if only to minimize the 'I told you so' smile playing on my husband's face. The answer from heaven came in the form of a name, a friend of mine with incredible baking expertise: Anna Fiona. I could outsource the job to her.

My objectives and vision did not have to be met by me. Why was I stressing about baking a cake when Anna Fiona was a baking ninja? Nervously, my unsteady fingers composed a short text message. Minutes later, I was breathing normally as I read her response, 'Yes, sure, I'll make the cake. Let's chat about what you want on Sunday and you can help me.'

Fast forward two weeks: Eliana's second birthday cake was complete. And it was stunning. I looked at the green and pink fondant icing draped over the butterfly-shaped vanilla sponge and admired the sparkly butterfly wings. This cake had been a team effort. Anna Fiona had enlisted her friend, Danielle, who had recently completed a cake-decorating course. The three of us spent an evening rolling, cutting and crafting. I had enjoyed learning a new skill. The resulting cake was a combination of Anna Fiona's exquisite baking skills, Danielle's technical brilliance and my eye for details. What a team. And it tasted delicious.

Created for community

We were all created for community, to live our lives with those around us, to love them and to learn from and with them. We are all created in God's image (Genesis 1:26). The Bible is full of small groups of people working together as God's image-bearers to take forward God's mission (Ruth and Naomi in the Old Testament book of Ruth, the twelve disciples throughout the Gospels, and Paul and Timothy in the Epistles are three examples). We weren't created to bake the cake alone. We belong to a community of faith. Mission needs to take place within that community, in the context of healthy relationships. For a perfect picture of what community should be, look at the picture of the Trinity: Father, Son and Holy Spirit, each with a different role, working together in unity.

Not only does community support us in mission but it acts as a magnet to draw others into the kingdom. Community living is missional. Just read the Acts of the Apostles to see the impact of a community living out Jesus-centred principles – thousands of people became Christians!

Who has God placed us in relationship with? How can we use our homes and hospitality to develop community? What does it mean to live generously, and how does community affect our children? These are some of the questions we will explore in this chapter. Let's start with one model of community: the Life Village.

The Life Village

The Life Village is a loving community invited by Azariah and me to be committed to each of our children, based on the African proverb 'It takes a village to raise a child'.

Before our daughter was born, Azariah and I realized that we would not have everything she needed for life. Who would teach her football, if that was what she liked, or how to run her own business? I have Malaysian heritage and my husband's family are from Nevis in the Caribbean. In these cultures whole communities gather round families to help bring them up. We felt this was what she needed, especially as neither of us had much close family. So we developed the idea of the Life Village – extended godparents – where we would invite people to become involved in the life of our child from birth to eighteen, offering what they could when they could – time, a skill, resources, prayer. These people would be the community surrounding Eliana, people we could draw on for wisdom and support. In time we hoped and prayed that she would have independent relationships with many of them. We couldn't bake this cake alone!

Both our children have Life Villages. We share our lives with these people. One member of Eliana's Life Village, Victoria, regularly writes her an encouraging letter which I print out and keep in a book. Others often come and spend an afternoon with her. One of Micah's favourite places to sit is at the piano, and recently one twelve-year-old member of his Life Village sat with him at the piano at church, letting him enjoy the music. Micah was delighted. Other members have offered their skills in drawing, sewing and reading, or their time, money or advice to enable our children to flourish.

As our children grow up, we pray that they would better understand the breadth and depth of God's love and the different aspects of God's character through the love they experience from these different people. We also pray that they would understand how they too are part of God's bigger story of mission in the world and have their own part to play.

The Life Village is an example of how our family has chosen to live out God's call for us to live in community. There are many other ways we can intentionally develop community around our families.

If we are looking to develop a mindset of community, where can we start? Let's stick with the baking theme and consider three ingredients for developing community: praying together, eating together and living life together.

Ingredient 1: Praying together

'If my people, who are called by my name, will humble themselves and pray and seek my face and turn from their wicked ways, then will I hear from heaven, and will forgive their sin and will heal their land' (2 Chronicles 7:14).

This passage from Chronicles reveals the power of praying together with others. God is responding to Solomon's prayer and declares that he will restore the people and the land after their time of distress if they pray and seek him humbly.[18] He promises to 'hear', 'forgive' and 'heal' – something that many of us long for as we pray for friends who don't know Jesus and for our communities that are in need of transformation.

Praying together is not always straightforward. We may worry that we don't sound holy enough or that we can't be honest when sharing our prayer needs. Praying with other people regularly about our own needs and our desires to see God's mission go forward may sound like a huge challenge if you've never done it before, but the impact it can have on our capacity to love others is massive.

Praying together can be as simple as praying with one or two Christian friends each week. My prayer partner, Claire, lives in Manchester so we talk and pray on the phone once a week about our own needs, the needs of our immediate family, and others in our God-given sphere of influence. One of the most powerful aspects of this has been the opportunity to humble myself and confess.

James 5:16 says: 'Therefore confess your sins to each other and pray for each other so that you may be healed.'

I tell Claire things I won't tell anyone else – personal issues and habits I am struggling with. Once I admitted to her that I found someone other than Azariah attractive. When I had confessed this to her, I realized it didn't feel like a burden I was carrying alone any more. I confessed it to God and over time the feelings faded and I spoke to Azariah about it. The confession was the path to healing.

Some of us may struggle with issues that are deeper, more painful and which need the help of professionals. Having a prayer partner won't necessarily solve problems overnight, but having close Christian friends who support us, in addition to the support of our husbands, is a way in which God will help us. What a privilege it is to have others who love us despite our mistakes and who can stand with us as we pray for our friends and neighbours to be drawn towards Jesus.

Real community is built on honesty. Do we have relationships where we can confess and hold one another accountable? Where we can pray with others for the mission that God has called us to? This needn't be with another mum. A retired person whose children have left home may be an excellent prayer partner. A younger single friend can bring a fresh perspective. These relationships take time to develop and need long-term investment but are the vital bedrock for mission. To put things bluntly, if I'm stressing about finding another man attractive, I'm hardly going to be focused on finding creative ways to bless my neighbour!

As I've spoken to mums about their prayer lives, I've been impressed with the variety of ways we find to pray for one another. Some people love to pray in groups that meet during the week with their toddlers, perhaps to delve into the Bible too. Others use prayer texts – sending prayer requests by text message and praying as they receive the text. Another idea is 'on the spot prayer': every time you meet with another Christian, simply praying briefly for one thing for each other, perhaps in the middle of the street, office or toddler group. What about setting an alarm on your phone twice a day to pray for your friend who is not yet a Christian?

We are making long-term investments when we seek to build prayerful relationships with one another. As Ruth, mum to Isla, six, Carys, three, and Keira, two, explains:

> What has inspired me to stick with my prayer triplet is the example of one of their mothers in our church. This mother prayed regularly at different times with two other mums who both died of cancer. She sat with them through their illness. These mums had shared life together. It has made me see that these friendships are for the long haul – they are not just people to share my life with now; they are the people who may share my death too. I want the kind of friends who will sit and hold my wasted hand as I lie dying, and I would gladly do the same for them.

Can we begin to imagine the supernatural impact that a praying community can have on the world around us? The lives

redeemed, the illnesses healed and the communities transformed? When we pray together with others and humbly seek
God's face, not only does God hear and respond to our requests
but something happens slowly in our hearts. We begin to understand and love each other more deeply. Our vision for mission
and our deepest desires become shared. It becomes less about
'my agenda' and more about how we as a praying community
all fit into God's bigger story of redemption. From experiencing
support within a praying community, we can begin to serve
together and open up our homes.

Ingredient 2: Eating together

> Share with the Lord's people who are in need. Practise hospitality.
> (Romans 12:13)

> Offer hospitality to one another without grumbling.
> (1 Peter 4:9)

Nick and Lucy Crawley's house is a place you want to be. Three
young people, a student and another couple sit around their
well-worn dark wood table with their four sons, aged eleven to
eighteen. Faces are happy, voices animated, and there is a sense
of family. Lucy brings out a sausage casserole, hot from the oven,
and as she places it on the table, we all dive in, helping ourselves
to the feast. More laughter, a joke or two, a story from one of
the boys and then we've begun. Nick reads a passage of Scripture;
we eat as we listen, discuss and then pray, with mouths full of
steaming meat and potatoes. This is church.

Nick and Lucy led our church in Bristol where we lived for
two years. Their church was based in several places throughout
those two years, including their home. Around their kitchen
table Azariah and I were discipled, challenged and prayed for.
Once, as Lucy iced a cake with her youngest son, I talked to her
about my life and she offered wise counsel. The Crawleys are

hospitable people and we were blessed to be part of their church community and to learn from and with them. We were welcomed into their family, to eat with them and with the church. Together we worshipped God around the kitchen table with others who had never experienced church before.

Author and missiologist Alan Hirsch says:

> People should be able to experience a foretaste of heaven from our families and our homes. This is where the church can rightly be viewed as a community of the redeemed, from all walks of life . . . Missional hospitality is a tremendous opportunity to extend the kingdom of God. We can literally eat our way into the kingdom of God.[19]

Not many churches meet around a kitchen table but, through hospitality, we can be the church to others as we eat together and use our homes (and perhaps our baking skills!) to demonstrate the love of God. Jesus was always eating with people (Mark 2:15–17; Luke 14:1–14; John 21:9–14) and often with people who were despised by the rest of society. He saw the value of sharing food. When I think of the gift of hospitality, I often think of sweating away in the kitchen cooking vats of chilli for insane numbers of people (can you tell that cooking isn't really my thing?). Despite my culinary skills, Azariah and I love welcoming people to our home and hearing their stories. We've had all sorts in our home – single-parent families, ex-alcoholics, people with special needs, students from India, elderly ladies with an axe to grind, lawyers and neighbours. Almost always, people are just grateful to be invited. God has been slowly peeling away my unhealthy desire to impress and instead encouraging me to allow people to see the real us. That often means a kitchen table covered in unopened bills and, like yesterday, Eliana's knickers lying in the middle of the hallway.

We've learned that hospitality doesn't have to be about mass catering and hard work. Friends of ours, Phil and Michelle, used to have a takeaway night every month where everyone would put in £5 and they'd get takeaway curry for everyone. They'd invite people from all aspects of their lives – church, work, neighbours. If takeaway nights and house parties aren't your thing, can you invite someone round who won't get invited to many other people's houses? Perhaps invite the mum whose child has ADHD for a play date? Or the mum with ADHD whose child has ADHD?! Or have the lonely elderly neighbour round for a cuppa and chat?

Ruth, mum to Zoe, four, and Phoebe, two, surprised everyone in the way she chose to use her home for hospitality:

> We held a Christmas party for all the children in Zoe's class at school. People asked, 'What does she want for a present?' and when I told them that it wasn't her birthday but that we just wanted to do it, they didn't get it. People thought it didn't make any sense. Why would you want twenty kids to come to your house, tread mud everywhere and wreck it, and not even bring a present? We just wanted people to come empty-handed and receive grace. I love the house full of kids and having nice, posh crisps. There's no pressure for a return invitation.

What a glorious image of God's kingdom this is! How can we take this principle of extending grace to people through our homes and apply it to our own situations? Our homes really can be places of immense blessing, no matter how small, messy or ill-equipped they are. How can we live hospitably in everything we do, willingly welcoming not only those who we know and love but also those who are different from us or marginalized by the rest of society? Here are some further ideas from other mums about how they use food and their homes to bless others:

- Take a meal, nappies or a DVD box set round to a mum who has just had a baby

- Give a little pamper pack, including a home-made cupcake, to a pregnant mum at the toddler group
- Invite mums from school round for coffee regularly
- Take round an Easter egg to your neighbours' house
- When you go shopping, take advantage of the 2-for-1 deals and donate the second item to a friend
- Make cakes for the school receptionist at the end of term: they often get forgotten
- Make gingerbread with your toddler and give it to a friend or work colleague
- Have a carol-singing and mulled wine party at Christmas for your neighbours
- Have a BBQ for your work colleagues in the summer or invite other children to come and play in the paddling pool or on the trampoline
- Use your home to host a craft evening where everyone brings a project they're working on and does it together
- Use your home to host a book club, toy swap or clothes swap
- If your flat is too small to host a party, invite your neighbours to a 'get to know you' party at the local café

Some of these ideas are pretty simple and can be a first step towards building relationships with those around us. However, hospitality is not always about the straightforward act of giving. Here's what Danielle, mum to Zion, ten, Judah, two, and Moses, four months, discovered:

> We used to have a homeless guy over to our place for a collective meal every Monday and then a Bible study. Everyone brought something. He brought a 2-litre bottle of Pepsi every week. At first I felt terrible that he wasted his money and that he couldn't afford it. Then the Lord reminded me, it's better to give than to receive, and that this man could and should contribute. And so, he took his bottle-collecting money and contributed to our

collective meal and, rather than being a homeless man who needed a meal, he was Joe, who brought the Pepsi. He was one of us. This power imbalance can be corrected as we learn to receive and not just give all the time.

I love this story from Danielle because it shows that hospitality is about giving and receiving. There is a mutuality in community. We sit round a common table and we enjoy the way God has made each one of us, regardless of social status. We all bring something – a story, some food, a prayer or challenge. We all go away richer, having experienced more of who God is. This is the kind of kingdom hospitality that God is calling us to. It can start with a meal, but it extends to our whole life.

Ingredient 3: Living life together

I have always been curious about the lives of those living in convents or monasteries. I visit a retreat centre every year and recently went to one where a group of nuns lived under the same roof, exercising gifts of hospitality, growing their own food and serving the local people. What would it mean for us as families with young children to open wide the doors of our homes and to invite others to come and live in our homes or closely alongside us, sharing not just meals but our day-to-day lives?

I know a number of people who are seeking to live missionally in this way.

Tony and Claire decided, when they got married, that they would live with another Christian couple, buy a house together and live in community. They pooled their resources, had regular hospitality evenings, prayed together and prioritized living ethically. Each couple then had one child and the couples were able to share their lives in practical ways through childcare, resources and babysitting. Their community house was a wonderful picture of holistic mission where what they ate and how they spent their money was an expression of worship just as much as the way in which they welcomed strangers into their home for meals.

Ed and Heidi, together with their single friend Tarn whom they had known for years, decided to set up a community house where they would foster vulnerable teenagers. Over a period of three years they have fostered one teenage boy and four teenage girls, one of whom they have just seen off to college. They have now also welcomed into their home a family with young children who are in transition. Tarn left the community home to get married to Murray. Tarn and Murray have now fostered a thirteen-month-old and a newborn with a view to adopting them.

These examples show the creativity that springs from community. Each 'community house' has a different flavour, but each resonates with the heart of God. Living together in community like this is counter-cultural and involves huge sacrifices and a totally different way of operating. Far from being 'perfect homes', these homes are places where I'm sure a lot of tears have been shed. Could God be calling us to live together in community with others in this way as an expression of love for our neighbour? Could this be a way in which we could welcome the lonely into families (Psalm 68:6) and care for orphans (James 1:27) or express something of the fullness of what it means to be good stewards of the earth?

Fostering or adoption is another way in which you could use your home to nurture community. My friend Sus fostered and then later adopted her daughter Kailey as a six-day-old baby. Sus was single at the time and living in the United States. Many of us want to wait for the 'perfect' timing or set of circumstances before we decide to opt for this level of community. But Sus had to face the reality that the perfect situation might never come. She says: 'I thought to adopt you needed to be married, with a big home and a better paid job. It was like a lightning bolt the day I realized those were good things to be waiting for, but that there were no guarantees of the "perfect situation" ever happening. I could spend my life waiting rather than doing.'

Sus then went through the long process of becoming an approved foster carer and adopted Kailey, having to continue working full-time when Kailey was still young. Not all families are called to foster or adopt children, but Sus is clear that as the body of Christ we are called to support and help those who are:

My community from church and family were champions of support. People showered me with clothes, nappies and everything I needed to turn my flat into 'baby land'. They babysat and cooked meals. Adoption might not be for everyone, but being supportive of people who do adopt *is* for everyone. Maybe it's because the Bible talks about us all being adopted into the Lord's family, or perhaps it is because we are encouraged as Christians to look after widows and orphans (or single mums in my case). I believe adoption should be at the heart of churches and Christian life.

Fostering and adopting is an incredible expression of God's missional heart. As an individual family you may feel totally overwhelmed by the idea of bringing a vulnerable young person into your home, but what if you knew there was a whole team of people at your church who were with you, ready to support you practically and through prayer? It is also possible to become a respite foster carer, which means offering a helping hand to full-time foster carers by providing short-term care in a safe and caring family home environment. If you know a foster carer or family who have adopted, perhaps you could offer to help them practically or commit to pray for them regularly?

Living life together by opening our home up to others looks different for all families. Here are some other suggestions for living life in community with others:

- Sharing babysitting with a group of other mums
- Asking teenagers you know to babysit and then forming a mentoring relationship with them

- Setting up a group of Christian mums who meet together regularly to pray and serve the community practically in some way
- Using your spare room for a lodger, a young person on a gap year or an international student
- Running a parenting group in your home with other Christian parents
- Welcoming your children's friends into your home
- Offering to care for your friends' and neighbours' pets while they're away
- Using your home to disciple people, for example, by inviting a younger Christian round to have tea with you each week and mentoring him/her

Living generously

'A generous person will prosper; whoever refreshes others will be refreshed' (Proverbs 11:25).

One way of applying some of the principles of living together in intentional community such as community homes or fostering and adopting is learning to be generous with what we have. To live in community with others means recognizing that our money and resources belong to God. We can use them to meet the needs of others. In our culture, materialism and consumerism is the dominant narrative. It takes guts to live counter-culturally in a generous way instead. A question we have been asking ourselves is, 'How can we as a family recognize the influence that money and possessions may have on our decisions and seek to align ourselves with God's view of money?' It is only when we recognize that all we have comes from God that we can start to be truly generous.

One step towards this could be to think of ways we can share our resources as a family. Perhaps we could invite our children's friends round to enjoy our treehouse, or lend our DIY tools so our neighbour can fix her fence? What about getting involved in a car pool or lending baby clothes to another mum? Perhaps our children could give some of their toys to a local family or post a home-made card or piece of artwork through a neighbour's door? Could we offer a cheap or free skill to others: music lessons, proofreading, babysitting or help setting up a website? We have discovered a great website called Streetbank (www.streetbank.com) which enables neighbours to share skills and equipment. Alternatively, we may want to give our family's resources and time to support a charity that tackles homelessness, cares for the environment or supports those with cancer.

Having a community mindset is not a comfortable thing. Are we prepared to sacrifice some of our privacy and individualism in order to experience the blessing of community, living our whole lives for God's kingdom, whatever that may look like?

The impact of community on our children

The people we surround ourselves with will have an impact on our children. Many of us have a protective instinct which will resist having more vulnerable people around our children. But not exposing our children to the wonder of different perspectives and types of people has negative repercussions too. Here's what Lizzie, mum to Caleb, four, and Joseph, two, says:

> We have a lot of people with substance misuse issues who come to our church. One week we ended up taking a man home in our car who we knew was homeless. He was lying in the road outside a shop and had had a lot to drink. We used it as an opportunity to talk to our son, Caleb, four, about what beer is and how, if you have too much, you get poorly. Of course we want to protect our children too, but these are people we love. Growing up, I had no awareness of poverty or addiction and I think that was a great shame. I want my kids to know about these things.

As our children grow, they will learn from those we have brought into their community as we live life alongside each other. If we decide to go as a family and take Christmas presents into the local school for children with disabilities, our children will begin to place value on those with disabilities. If we decide to take an elderly neighbour some warm slippers in winter, it sends a powerful message to our children. They will learn about the nature of God from those we pray with, eat with and live alongside and from those we invite into our home and share our resources and time with. By committing to live in community with others, we are laying foundations for our children that will stand them in good stead for the future.

Committing to community

God has given us all opportunities to share our lives with others, whether that's through prayer, hospitality, babysitting, fostering, living generously or creating a Life Village for our children.

As we commit to sharing life with whomever God has placed us in relationship with, let's pray that we see God bring transformation in our own lives as well as those around us. Let's pray that all we have and all we are will point to Jesus and that our children would discover what it means for them to play their part in God's mission. Let's commit to baking our cakes together and making them beautiful.

Questions for exploration

1. Who has God placed your family in relationship with at the moment who could support you in mission and pray with and for you? How could these relationships be even more enriching?
2. What level of hospitality are you happy with and what is 'out of your comfort zone'? Where is God challenging you as a family?
3. What is one way in which you could live more generously with what you have as a family? Take one step towards this goal this week.

EPILOGUE: LET IT BE SO . . .

Enlarge the place of your tent,
    stretch your tent curtains wide,
    do not hold back;
lengthen your cords,
    strengthen your stakes.
For you will spread out to the right and to the left;
    your descendants will dispossess nations
    and settle in their desolate cities.
(Isaiah 54:2–3)

When I (Joy) stood on a stage in 1999 and proclaimed these words at a prayer meeting, at first I couldn't understand why people laughed. Soon, I realized they were laughing because I was seven months pregnant and wearing an enlarged and tent-like maternity dress. At that time, I was a physical embodiment of the passage I was reading from.

These words rang true for me on that day, and it is our prayer that they ring true for you now. It is also our prayer that you will embody those words, wherever you are and whatever it is that your life looks like on this day.

It is our prayer that your sphere of influence will be enlarged, that you will be stretched and opened up, that you will not hold back, that you will be lengthened and strengthened, and that through all of this, God's kingdom will grow, and that through his power at work in you, desolate places will become vibrant again.

Here is our 'Amen', our 'Let it be':

Let there be hope rising within you as you dream new
    dreams,
  let there be anticipation, passion and vision.
Let there be a safe place that holds and nurtures you,
  may you know what it is to be loved.
Let there be a mending of broken hearts,
  may you shake off the heavy loads that have held you back,
  and sweep leaves from the path for others.
Let there be solid ground beneath your feet,
  may you build on firm foundations.
Let there be laughter, celebration and joy.
Let there be parties and candles, beaches, woods,
  adventures, traditions, chuckles, bandaged knees,
  and ice-cream at the end of the day.
Let there be rest and peace,
  may you be restored, recreated,
  held in a rhythm that sustains and renews.
Let there be stories and breathless, incredulous wonder
    anew!
May you dare to go, step into the new and realize that you
    are not alone,
  for he is already there.
May you come to the end of your own resources.
  Let there be others who have gone before.
May you grind to a halt, may you be empty.
  May you begin to plumb the fathomless depths of grace in
    that moment.

May you drink good coffee and laugh until there are tears.
  Let there always be another alongside you in storms or
    sunshine.
May you know the strength and joy that rises
  when you serve shoulder to shoulder with a sister.
Let there be reality and authenticity.
  May you keep standing through it all.
Let there be weakness, let there be strength.
Let there be friends! Let there be food!
  Let there be late-night soul-searching and midday picnic fun.
Let there be invitation, let there be challenge, let truth rule, and
    grace reign.
  May we be known, yet loved,
  and may we love and learn from others.
Let us go!
  Let us not be defined by parameters of comfort and safety!
Let us be bringers of hope, light and kindness, bearers of peace.
  Let us serve with compassion and casseroles.
May we place limits on our judgment,
  but never on our love.
Let us dream, release vision,
  may we plant and see shoots.
Let it be so!
Amen.

APPENDIX

Blogs

http://thevicarswife.wordpress.com
The vicar's wife writes useful things about how to communicate the gospel to children.

http://tanyamarlow.com
Tanya Marlow writes about character, calling and living with illness.

http://annarobbo.wordpress.com
Anna Robinson writes about life as a family on mission.

http://alphamothernomore.wordpress.com
Joy blogs here about family life and mission.

http://www.aholyexperience.com
Ann Voskamp is a Canadian farmer's wife who wrote the *New York Times* bestseller *One Thousand Gifts*. She home-schools her six children, and writes about giving thanks in the everyday.

Discipleship resources

Soul Food for Mums: A Weekly Devotional for Baby's First Year by Lucinda van der Hart and Anna France-Williams (IVP, 2011)

www.moravian.org/faith-a-congregations/moravian-daily-texts/daily-texts.html
Daily prayer emails

www.licc.org.uk
The London Institute of Contemporary Christianity sends out a devotional email every day.

www.rejesus.co.uk
This website includes a spirituality zone, which includes a link to daily prayer resources.

www.churchofengland.org/prayer-worship/join-us-in-daily-prayer.aspx
This is the link to the Church of England website, where the daily office can be followed online every day.

www.captivatedmums.org.uk
Captivated is a gathering of mums who are passionate about pursuing God. The Facebook group (captivatedmums) is a helpful place to find encouragement, advice and prayer. Captivated also holds an annual conference.

Discipleship resources for children

www.jesusstorybookbible.com
The Jesus Storybook Bible by Sally-Lloyd Jones and illustrated by Jago (Zondervan, 2012)
This Bible for 4–8 year olds is beautifully written and illustrated and invites children to discover for themselves that Jesus is at the centre of God's great story of salvation and at the centre of their story, too.

www.godventure.co.uk
Fun, creative and seasonal resources to help families explore the Bible and prayer

http://flamecreativekids.blogspot.co.uk/
Creative children's ministry ideas from Mina Munns

http://thedailydoughnut.com/
Bite-size Bible study for all the family

www.childrenswork.co.uk
This magazine contains ideas, resources and guidance for Christian children's leaders. It also includes lots of ideas for families wanting to connect with God.

Pens – Bible devotions for 3–6 year olds, published by CWR
Topz – Bible devotions for 7–11 year olds, published by CWR
YPs – Bible devotions for 11–15 year olds, published by CWR

Beginning with God – Bible-reading notes for pre-schoolers, published by the Good Book Company

www.scriptureunion.org.uk
Check out Scripture Union for resources aimed at children of all ages.

www.thebiblecurriculum.com
This website provides a seven-year programme for teaching the Bible to primary-aged children in a church setting. Resources can be bought online in a 'Pay as you teach' format.

http://www.seedsfamilyworship.net
Children's worship album and ideas for family worship

http://www.adventuresoftoby.com/
Films and books about the adventures a little boy goes on when he meets Jesus

Courses

http://www.relationshipcentral.org/marriage-course
The Marriage Course – courses run in churches designed to give your marriage an MOT

http://www.relationshipcentral.org/parenting-children-course
The Parenting Children Course is for any parents, step-parents, prospective parents or carers of children aged 0–10 years.

http://www.relationshipcentral.org/parenting-teenagers-course
The Parenting Teenagers Course is for any parents, step-parents, or carers of children aged 11–18 years.

http://www.careforthefamily.org.uk
Marriage by Design DVD and discussion book by Care for the Family
21st Century Marriage DVD by Care for the Family
21st Century Family DVD by Care for the Family

http://www.new-wine.org/resources/family-time
Family Time is a collection of resources providing tools, practical advice and support to parents of children and teenagers. The Parenting Children and Parenting Teenagers Course resources are available from this website.

Campaigns and charities

www.28toomany.org
28 Too Many is a values-based charity funded by supporters and donations, created to help eradicate Female Genital Mutilation (FGM) in the twenty-eight countries within Africa where it is still practised.

http://www.homeforgood.org.uk/campaign/
Home for Good is a national campaign which aims to make fostering and adoption a normal part of Church life.

www.streetbank.com
Streetbank shows you all the things and skills your neighbours are offering. Sign up and get connected to your neighbourhood.

www.baby-basics.org.uk
Baby Basics is a Sheffield-based organization which provides essential clothes and baby equipment to vulnerable families.

NOTES

1. Based on a definition given by Stuart Murray, in *Church Planting: Laying Foundations* (Paternoster Press, 1998), p. 31.
2. 'Messy Church' is a once-a-month time of worship, creativity and eating together for families who might not usually go to a mainstream church service. There are now over 1,700 Messy Churches meeting around the world. For more information, see www.messychurch.org.uk.
3. D. W. Winnicott, 'Primary Maternal Preoccupation', in P. Mariotti (ed.), *The Maternal Lineage: Identification, Desire, and Transgenerational Issues* (Routledge, 2012), pp. 59–66.
4. Sue Gerhardt, *Why Love Matters: How Affection Shapes a Baby's Brain* (Brunner-Routledge, 2004).
5. Tim Keller and Kathy Keller, *The Meaning of Marriage* (Hodder and Stoughton, 2011), p. 117.
6. Nicky and Sila Lee, *The Marriage Book* (Alpha International Resources, 2009), pp. 32–33.
7. Compassion's child sponsorship programme provides children living in poverty in the developing world with education, healthcare, supplemental nutrition, and opportunities to hear and respond to the gospel. See www.compassionuk.org.
8. Keller and Keller, *Meaning of Marriage*, p. 235
9. http://www.patheos.com/blogs/whatshesaid/2012/03/relationship-tweets-from-the-worlds-oldest-living-married-couple/ 1 March 2012.
10. *How to Be a Good Mother* with Sharon Horgan, first shown on Channel 4, 11 January 2012.
11. *Pocket Oxford Dictionary*, 7th edn (Clarendon Press, 1986).
12. *Common Worship: Services and Prayers for the Church of England* (Church House Publishing, 2000), p. 165.
13. Sally Lloyd-Jones, Jago (illustrator), *The Jesus Storybook Bible: Every Story Whispers His Name* (Zondervan, 2007).
14. See Isaiah 6:8.
15. Dallas Willard, *Renovation of the Heart: Putting on the Character of Christ* (IVP, 2002), p. 116.
16. E. Moltmann-Wendell, *The Women around Jesus* (SCM Press, 1982), pp. 22, 27.
17. Ann Morton Voskamp, *One Thousand Gifts* (Zondervan, 2010).
18. *Asbury Bible Commentary*, www.biblegateway.com.
19. Alan Hirsch and Lance Ford, *Right Here, Right Now: Everyday Mission for Everyday People* (Shapevine, 2011), p. 203.

Lucinda van der Hart
& Anna France-Williams

A weekly devotional for baby's 1st year

related titles from IVP

Soul Food for Mums

*A weekly devotional
for baby's 1st year*
Lucinda van der Hart
& Anna France-Williams

ISBN: 978-1-84474-521-0
232 pages, paperback

You are too exhausted to think, never mind pray, your home is a mess and you can't find your Bible …

Soul Food will nourish you through your baby's first year, offering inspirational and practical ideas for applying God's Word and incorporating prayer into your daily life. It won't make you feel guilty about the time or energy you simply don't have.

With honesty and humour, the authors draw upon their own, and others', experiences of motherhood. The result is both delightful and unusual.

Succinct, accessible, weekly biblical reflections. A lifeline for every mother with a new baby.

*'Can be nibbled at or devoured for spiritual nourishment …
A lovely book.'* Amy Boucher Pye

'Will connect you in new ways with God's heart.' Sammy Greig

*'… will help mothers hold on to the Lord, glimpse the wonder
of life and keep growing as Christian disciples.'* Amy Orr-Ewing

*'A most excellent and valuable addition to the bedside table
of any expectant or new mother.'* Sarah Wynter

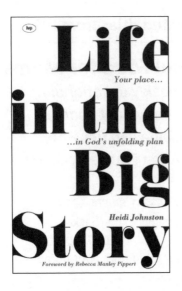

Life in the Big Story

Your place in God's unfolding plan

Heidi Johnston

ISBN: 978-1-84474-579-1
192 pages, paperback

We are part of an epic story. From Adam and Eve as they walked with God, to the charged anticipation of the Israelites as they prepared to enter the Promised Land; from the life, death and resurrection of Jesus to the birth of the church and beyond, God's plan for his people remains constant.

Life in the Big Story is a call to find our place in God's story. It is a call to hear his heartbeat and let it change our own.

Without knowing him, without seeing his heart as it beats on every page from Genesis to Revelation, we will never understand what we are called to be.

But when we do, we will catch a glimpse of something bigger than the lives we settle for. We will be drawn to delve deeper into God's Word, discovering for ourselves the joy of knowing the God who calls us his own. As the people of a holy Lord, we will be challenged to live lives worthy of his name.

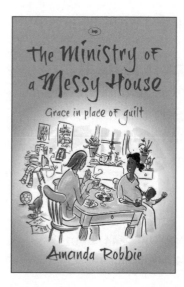

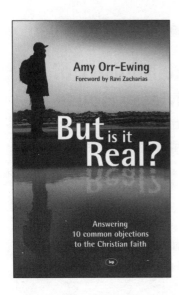

God Doesn't Do Waste

Redeeming the whole of life
Dave Bookless

ISBN: 978-1-84474-473-2
160 pages, paperback

Meet 'the Bookless bunch', a very ordinary family who went green. When God challenged him over his attitude to the environment, Dave Bookless did a total rethink. This led to major changes, not only in his family's lifestyle but also eventually in his career: full-time involvement in the global A Rocha movement that aims to care for God's fragile world.

But in one sense this book isn't about going green at all. It's a personal account of a life lived in relationship. It's about roots and belonging, suffering and healing, identity and meaning, faith and doubt. It's about how in God's economy nothing need be wasted.

This is a story about the messiness that each human being wades through in every area of their lives, and about a God who can take all that seems most wasteful and useless, and recycle it into something of infinite worth.

Inter-Varsity Press

For more information about IVP
and our publications visit

www.ivpbooks.com

Get regular updates at **ivpbooks.com/signup**
Find us on **facebook.com/ivpbooks**
Follow us on **twitter.com/ivpbookcentre**

Inter-Varsity Press, a company limited by guarantee registered in England and Wales, number 05202650. Registered
office IVP Bookcentre, Norton Street, Nottingham NG7 3HR, United Kingdom. Registered charity number 1105757.